Exhibitions

EXHIBITIONS

an exhibitor's guide

PETER COTTERELL

Hodder & Stoughton
LONDON SYDNEY AUCKLAND

British Library Cataloguing in Publication Data

Cotterell, Peter
  Exhibitions
  I. Title
  659.152

  ISBN 0-340-56793-7

First published 1992

Produced by Serif Tree, Kidlington, Oxon
Printed in Great Britain for the education publishing
division of Hodder & Stoughton Ltd, Mill Road, Dunton Green,
Sevenoaks, Kent by St Edmundsbury Press Ltd.

CONTENTS

ACKNOWLEDGEMENTS

Many people assist in the writing of a book.

Those who most knew they were helping were my long-suffering family, Pauline, Malcolm and Owen who put up with a table strewn with scribblings, and a scribe with a short fuse. Also long-suffering was my typist Margaret Fitch, the only one who could read my writing. Thank you.

Help was also given by a number of UK friends with whom dialogue has clarified some thoughts and added others over the years. Thank you Alfred Alles, Frank Blake, Gordon Carlton, Malcolm Cook, Paul Holmes, Richard John, Jack Jones, Steve Kingshott, Philip Kleinman, Bob Kyte, Mel Lewis, Bill Levell, Jocelyn Marsh, David Nathan, Roy Price, Bill Richards, Patsy Roberston, Frank Rose, Owen Spence, Jo Thompson, Maria Totman, Stewart Vassie, Rex Walden, Malcolm Whitmarsh, Jim Wiseman and Peter Worger.

In the USA I would like to thank Ed Chapman, Bill Chipping, Susan Friedman, Fred Fox, Scott Gray, Darlene Gudea, Gerry Kallman, Jane Lorimer, Bill Mee, Steve Miller, Donna Sanford and Don Walter. And, in Australia, Mike and Val Sedin. Here's a handshake across the miles.

The publishers would like to thank the following for giving permission to reproduce copyright material in this book:

The National Exhibition Centre, Birmingham (p. 4); Labmate (p. 10); the Royal Agricultural Society press office (p. 12); Angex Ltd (p. 13); the British Public Works Association (p. 18); Incentive Magazine (p. 20); Novotel London, Hammersmith International Centre (p. 24); the London International Book Fair (p. 69); Sopexa Ltd, London (p. 57); the Birmingham Post and Mail Ltd (p. 77); Food from Britain (p. 98).

PREFACE

This book has been written by an exhibitor. Being as it is a book for practitioners, written by a practitioner, it doesn't puff the exhibition industry. It tells it like it is. And it doesn't pull any punches.

If it has a bias, it is biased towards the exhibitor. If it has a common thread it is that exhibitions work best when they fulfil defined sales and marketing goals, rather than those concerned with corporate ego. If it has targets to attack then these are the die-hard bad habits and practices of an industry, which, in the words of a famous politician has never had it so good. Until now, perhaps?

And if it shoots the odd sacred cow or two? Well, that's what a good book is supposed to do.

Peter Cotterell
National Exhibitors Association
1992

THE

EXHIBITION

BUSINESS

Exhibitions of one kind or another have a pedigree and history stretching back almost to the dawn of mankind. Our need to trade has brought with it an understandable need for sellers and buyers to meet.

A loose definition of exhibitions calls them 'occasional collections of sellers and buyers brought together for the benefit of both'. Traditional street markets, held on set days, are the forerunners of the modern exhibition.

Whereas street markets are aimed at the people in the street, exhibitions, in terms of organised consumer events, aim to discriminate. A boat show or garden show aims to attract only those interested in boats or gardens.

The trade exhibition, the main subject of this book, discriminates further and aims to attract only buyers from a defined trade or industry – a travel show for travel agents, a building show for those in the building trade, and so on.

The exhibition business in the UK has five main categories of people involved in it. These are:

1 *Visitors* Without visitors, in sufficient numbers and with sufficient buying power, an exhibition cannot function. Visitors are the most important people in the industry.

2 *Exhibitors* The reason the visitors come; the second most important people in the industry.

3 *Organisers* The companies and entrepreneurs who make it happen; the creators of the event and the risk-takers.

4 *Contractors and suppliers* The organisations working for exhibitors and organisers to build, stage and help promote the exhibits and the event.

5 *Hall owners* The people who own the exhibition halls and open spaces where exhibitions are held.

Structure of the exhibition industry

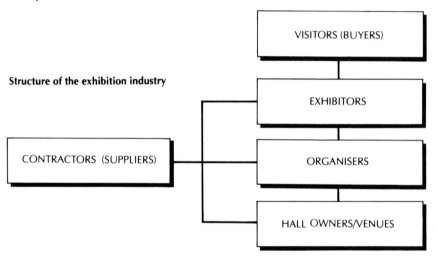

In terms of jobs, those wishing to work in the industry have a wide choice and can choose between being exhibitors, organisers, contractors, suppliers or venue managers. In terms of the jobs available, those working for exhibitors will probably handle the exhibition function as a part-time aspect of a sales, marketing or PR job. There are very few full-time exhibition specialists in UK companies.

Those working for contractors or suppliers could be electricians, carpet fitters, plumbers or carpenters as well as marketing consultants, stand designers, publicity experts or audio-visual specialists. The field is broad. Organisers employ sales people to sell exhibition space, administrators to set up and run their operations and marketing managers to promote. Venue managers employ sales people to sell their space to organisers, administrators to oversee events going on and technicians.

The last three decades have been important ones for the UK exhibition industry, now said to be worth nearly £1 billion in terms of expenditure by UK companies. In this time the amount of covered exhibition space available has increased dramatically with the setting-up and growth of one major centre, the National Exhibition Centre in Birmingham, and others in Wembley, Glasgow, London, Manchester, Brighton, Harrogate and Bournemouth. Also in this period the proportion of promotional budgets spent by exhibiting companies on UK events has moved from around four per cent to around eight per cent although, at the time of writing (1992) this surge seemed to have peaked.

There may be a number of reasons for this apparent flattening of growth. Recession, affecting most of industry, also affects exhibitions, often barometers of the economic strength of their industries. Exhibitors are now more likely to be selective, being more aware of the strengths and weaknesses of the medium and therefore less likely to exhibit lavishly just to 'fly the flag', as in the 60s and 70s. Another important factor which cannot be ignored is the impact of the EC on the UK market, with exhibitors being lured into spending their exhibition budgets in Paris or Frankfurt, rather than London or Birmingham.

The last few years have been a period of enforced change for the exhibition business. Union 'closed shops', once so powerful in the industry, became illegal in 1991. And 1992 will see the passing of official orders to curb the monopolistic practices of some hall-owners, organisers and contractors. An embarrassing corruption trial in 1991 resulted in the imprisonment of two senior executives, one for giving bribes, one for receiving.

Recent years have also seen a number of initiatives by the beneficiaries of exhibitor spend (the venue owners, organisers and contractors), to try and increase that spend with questionable results. The Exhibition Export Council was started by the Association of Exhibition Organisers in 1986 to promote overseas events and died quietly in 1988 after only two exhibitors joined. Then came the Exhibition Industry Federation (EIF) which was a collection of hall-owners, organisers and contractors which undertook quantitative research into the industry. Currently the EIF has lost two of its three financial backers, the organisers and contractors. Hoping to fill its place was – now Moribund – the Exhibition Marketing Group, another collection of organisers and hall owners formed in 1991 and dedicated to promoting exhibitions as the best way marketing managers can spend their budgets. Such obviously partisan initiatives are

The National Exhibition Centre, Birmingham

generally disregarded by serious exhibitors, who prefer to be guided by the evidence of their own experience and by their own judgement.

Despite some concerted lobbying, Westminster has remained impervious to pleas that UK exhibitions should be subsidised from the public coffers, as they are in Germany. Indeed the Department of Trade and Industry (DTI) recently withdrew a subsidy once paid to exhibition organisers promoting their UK events to potential overseas visitors. However, incoming groups of specific buyers and press are still arranged by trade associations and organisers and subsidised by the Department of Trade and Industry.

It is trite but probably true to say that in the 1990s the exhibition industry stands at a cross roads. Behind it are the successes, and excesses of the last 30 years. Ahead lies an economy injured by recession, a whole new breed of more knowledgeable exhibitors, official bodies that will be watching carefully for any slipping back into bad old habits and the uncertainties of a Europe attempting cohesion against a world trend of fragmentation.

It's going to be an interesting time, so read on.

Points for Discussion

1 What are the five main categories of people involved in the exhibition business?

2 Which is the most important group and why?

3 Why do you think Birmingham was chosen as the site for the National Exhibition Centre?

4 What venues for exhibitions are available in your area?

5 What other reasons could account for the slow down in the growth of the exhibition industry?

6 What arguments could be made for, and against subsidising the UK exhibition industry from public funds?

CHAPTER TWO

THE

NATURE OF

EXHIBITIONS

For the marketing manager, exhibitions represent one of many ways of promoting products or services. Direct mail, advertising, public relations, sponsorship, corporate hospitality and open days are all other, arguably more effective ways in which marketing budgets can be spent. Exhibitions can be a very expensive exercise not least in terms of management time and the cost of having highly paid members of the sales force off the road. Exhibitors should multiply the cost of the space by at least four and up to ten times to arrive at a true total. Nevertheless exhibitions offer a number of unique benefits not enjoyed by other media:

- **The buyer comes to the seller** No other medium delivers the market in quite the same way as an exhibition. Many companies find that the time and travel saved by having customers and potential customers come to them is well worth the expense. Some companies have even dispensed with a traditional sales force and use exhibitions to make all their contacts.

- **A lot of buyers come to sellers** One exhibition organiser estimates that his exhibitors collect six months worth of sales leads in the four days of his show. Certainly more potential business could be passing the stand in those few short days than the sales force will see in the rest of the year.

● **Known decision makers attend**   Research indicates that 29% of exhibition visitors are from senior management. A show is a unique opportunity to meet those decision-makers to whom the sales force are normally denied access. For the record, 51% come from middle management and 84% have a buying influence of some kind.

● **Even new prospects attend**   Over one third of exhibition visitors are new to their job or new to their industry. This is understandable since, for the uninitiated, an exhibition represents a chance to quickly gather a large amount of information about the market.

● **The contact is face-to-face**   Most companies cannot begin the selling process seriously until a face-to-face contact is made. Advertising, PR, direct mail, telesales etc. can raise awareness and interest but it is usually the physical meeting of buyer and seller that accelerates the process of obtaining an order. Many companies find that exhibitions are their real point of sale.

● **Hard-to-see buyers can be seen**   There is no appointment to be made, no secretary to convince. The buyers are just a few feet away.

● **Exhibition visitors are responsive**   An exhibition is the only medium that appeals to all five senses, and visitors walk round shows in a kind of heightened awareness. They are more responsive to new ideas than when in their offices and, unlike any other sales medium, have deliberately set aside time to come and learn. Advertising in the press, on radio or TV is intrusive on the buyer's time. So is direct mail or a sales person's cold call or telephone call. At an exhibition, the buyer has voluntarily set aside time to be sold to.

● **Business ambience is right**   The exhibition stand can be a perfect place from which to do business. It is like a temporary sales showroom but more neutral, with the buyer feeling more at ease. It is neither exclusively the sellers' home-ground nor the buyers', with advantages to both.

● **Exhibitions are a stage**   The stand is a temporary showcase for products or services. Stunning visual impact can be achieved with light, colour and movement, with a breadth and scope just not possible from a briefcase. The full range of theatrical elements can be brought into play and used to significant advantage.

● **No other medium comes as close** An exhibition provides an environment for products needing demonstrations. Hands-on experience can be offered, products can be touched, heard, smelt, tasted as well as seen working. No other medium gets the products so close to its market.

● **Exhibition visitors are captive** An exhibitor has a relatively captive audience. There are no telephones ringing, no heads round office doors with urgent requests. Generally, the attention is undivided.

● **Fulfilment is possible** If a prospect's interest is stimulated by a magazine advertisement, editorial, TV advertisement, direct mail piece or telephone call, there is a delay in getting further information. In the show environment, curiosity can be immediately satisfied. Interest can be turned quickly into a buying desire and even into an order.

● **Information is instantly available** In the field, technical questions about the product may have to be referred back to the company by the sales staff. On the stand, technical experts can be on hand to answer questions as they arise.

● **Test marketing is meaningful** Test marketing can be very expensive. An exhibition can offer a cost-effective way of researching new markets and getting the facts. New markets, both demographic and geographic can be investigated and many companies rightly use overseas exhibitions as their first step into export. Another significant advantage is that new products or services can be offered at prototype stage and some instant feedback obtained directly from the marketplace.

● **Sales leads can be cheaper** Many exhibitors with a grasp of the art now find their events to be the cheapest way to generate vital sales leads. The costs of capitalising on the chances can be significantly lower than gathering leads by advertising, direct mail, telesales, the sales force or any other method.

This is not to say that these are the only benefits to be gained from an exhibition. The event might revitalise the sales force. Opportunities for press coverage and corporate hospitality might present themselves. High-quality lists of visitors might be given free, or sold at low-cost by the organiser. Business might be done with other exhibitors and information might emerge about a competitor.

It is vital that, in order to maximise the benefit of all these advantages, a logical and clear-headed approach is made to the business of exhibiting. Woolly objectives such as 'we're there to fly the flag' or 'we're exhibiting because our competitors are there' can doom the enterprise to failure.

In the first instance the key reason for being at the show must be identified and this is usually 'to get sales leads' or, less commonly, 'to get orders'. In both cases a simple calculation of the total cost per sales lead, or cost per order will produce a figure, albeit a crude one, which can be used to measure one show against another, and more importantly, the effectiveness of exhibitions against other forms of lead or order generation. If the event can pay for itself in terms of leads and orders then any further less easily measured benefits are a bonus.

Types of exhibition

Exhibitions can be described as international, national, regional or local, depending on their catchment area for visitors and exhibitors. The aspirations of their organisers may also play a part. Up until quite recently in the UK almost any event could be termed 'International' if a certain percentage of the organiser's visitor promotional budget was spent in overseas markets. Since much of this money was, until 1990, supplied by the British Overseas Trade Board (BOTB), many shows were able to acquire a cosmopolitan flavour for little effort.

By the same token UK shows are often described as 'National' when in reality they draw the overwhelming majority of their visitors, if not exhibitors, from a radius of one hundred miles or less.

Currently there is no formal agreement on terms.

Consumer and trade events

Most exhibitions with which readers are concerned will fall into the category of 'consumer' or 'trade' events. Consumer events are set up so

A trade exhibition

that organisations can sell to the public. Garden shows, homeshows, antique fairs, boat shows and careers conventions would group under this heading.

Trade events are staged so that organisations can sell to other organisations – business selling to business. This is the largest category and the one on which this book concentrates. Industrial events, exhibitions aimed at retailers and wholesalers, and events for the professions (doctors, solicitors, accountants) would all come into this category. There are very few 'trades' which do not have their own commercial event.

Some events mix the trade and consumer elements, catering for both types of visitor. Agricultural shows, also called 'county' shows are a good example, attracting both the farming fraternity and the general public. Some computer events and motor shows also serve both markets.

Other events

There are other types of exhibition. There is a growing awareness of the effectiveness of the private exhibition or travelling roadshow, whereby one organisation exhibits its products or services to an invited audience of trade buyers. Such organisations may also allow other non-competing or complementary organisations to share the activity. Roadshows are popular ways of selling to retailers in a defined geographic area.

Also worthy of note are the world fairs or Expo's where countries will take space to increase awareness of their existence, culture and industrial capabilities, in order to improve tourism, trade or just friendship between nations. On a lesser scale are the great national exhibitions where one country will stage an event to showcase its achievements and invite the outside world.

Classification of trade exhibitions

Attempts have been made to classify trade events into 'vertical' and 'horizontal'. The exhibitors as well as the visitors at an event may be described in these terms.

An exhibition for hoteliers where suppliers of food, catering equipment, computer equipment and services, furnishings, telecommunications and

An agricultural show

The Ideal Home Exhibition is one of several national exhibitions staged at Earls Court

Horizontal and vertical classification of exhibitions

INDUSTRIES

VISITORS: A B C D E F G H

EXHIBITORS: 1 2 3 4 5 6 7 8

INDUSTRIES

i Horizontal exhibitors, horizontal visitors

ii Horizontal exhibitors, vertical visitors

iii Vertical exhibitors, horizontal visitors

iv Vertical exhibitors, vertical visitors

note: Visitors can also be 'verticalised' when selected by job function, ie an event may be aimed at sales directors, financial controllers, production managers, safety officers etc from a range of industries.

uniforms were all under one roof could be described as 'horizontal' in that the exhibitors are drawn from a broad spectrum of business. The visitor profile however, since the visitors are all hoteliers and from no other trade, could be described as 'vertical'. This would be an example of a 'horizontal exhibitor/vertical visitor' event.

Further specialisation could take place by running a 'uniforms for hoteliers' event which would be classified as 'vertical exhibitor/vertical visitor' since both buyers and sellers are drawn from a single 'trade'.

If the uniforms event was broadened out into 'uniforms for business' then this would be an example of a 'vertical exhibitors/horizontal visitors' exhibition. The exhibitors would all be in the business of making all types of uniforms and the visitors would come from a broad range of organisations using them such as hotels, banks, retailers security companies etc.

The last category of show would be the general trade and industry 'business to business' event where a range of different organisations, such as printers, publicity companies, insurance companies and office equipment dealers are presented to a general business audience, often small businesses. Such events are classed as 'horizontal exhibitors/horizontal visitors' and are often put on by local authorities and chambers of commerce to provide a business focus for their region or town.

Confusion is sometimes introduced when even further specialisation termed 'verticalisation' occurs. 'Computer software for hoteliers' might justifiably be classified as a 'vertical exhibitor/vertical visitor' event. It could also be argued that 'software for hotel sales' or 'computers in hotel catering' may, by their further specialisation, make the first examples look horizontal by comparison.

Points for Discussion

1 What are the key reasons for an exhibitor to attend an exhibition?

2 What benefits can an exhibition offer to an exhibitor?

3 Why do agricultural shows mix elements of both consumer and trade events?

4 Classify exhibitions recently staged at venues in your area as vertical or horizontal with respect to both visitors and exhibitors.

CHAPTER THREE

CHOOSING AN EXHIBITION

An appreciation of the nature of exhibitions, the types available and the objectives to be met are all vital considerations when selecting an event in which to participate. A certain amount of cynicism might also be an asset, as in any buying situation.

Clearly, the choice will first be governed by the geographical trading area of the organisation and its aspirations. Some exhibitors will concentrate on events in their region, whilst others will exhibit to open up a new territory or country. After that, and the obvious choice of trade or consumer event, the options will often include horizontal and vertical events.

The trend over the last decade (1981–1991) has been an increasing verticalisation or specialisation of events. For many organisations, in many industries this has been a worthwhile change of direction. A specialised show will generally deliver the specialists; those serious buyers who concentrate on a narrow defined area.

It should be remembered, however, that many buyers are generalists and may not want to spend a valuable day or half-day visiting an event which only covers a small part of their total buying remit. Additionally, those executives, especially at senior level, who make the buying decisions but have others to issue the orders, may well prefer to spend their time at a broad-based event where a range of possibilities can be looked at under one roof.

To use our example in the previous chapter the general manager of a hotel may well attend a broad-based show featuring a wide range of goods and

THE 1992 MOBILE CRANE AND MATERIALS HANDLING EXHIBITION

NATIONAL EXHIBITION CENTRE BIRMINGHAM

AMCM

ASSOCIATION OF MOBILE CRANE MANUFACTURERS

A typical exhibition brochure

services supplied to hoteliers but would probably send the sales manager to 'software for hotel sales'.

A highly specialised show will often attract specialists from within large companies and this is well and good if such people are the main target. However, medium-sized and small organisations which may also be important to the exhibitor, may not be able to afford the luxury of such specialists and may therefore not attend.

Vertical events can also die quickly for regular exhibitors who find that they are talking to the same visitors year after year. Visitors may also find that the exhibitor mix is unchanged. The small, specialised show can also be more vulnerable to recession than the bigger horizontal event.

The motivation for the event

Shows are not always staged by their organisers as a direct means of raising revenue, although most events have to run at a profit or die. Events are sometimes put on to fulfil other objectives, sometimes with disastrous results. As an example, the ill-fated 'Festival of London' which collapsed in July 1989 owing over £1 million was staged largely because the management of Alexandra Palace wanted a big event to showcase the venue following its expensive refurbishment after a fire. The 'Festival of Birmingham' due to run in the summer of 1990 was also cancelled, depriving the council owned National Exhibition Centre (NEC) of a lucrative and prestigious happening during the 'quiet' season.

Many exhibition venues, such as the NEC and Earls Court and Olympia have their own organising companies whose priority is not unnaturally, to fill the empty spaces. Obviously, this does not always work in the best interests of the exhibitor. As another example, Philbeach Events, an organising company owned by P & O's Earls Court and Olympia, only run events in their owner's venues. In 1990 Philbeach launched a summer event called 'Lifestyles 2000', which flopped, resulting in many exhibitors complaining of substantial losses.

Trade exhibitions mounted by venues themselves should therefore be treated with some caution. The benefits to the halls may be measured in the *quantity* of visitors that turn up and pay for car-parking, catering and cloakroom tickets, rather than the *quality* of those that attend. For this

Thousands of business people visit Incentive every year. It's the largest and most comprehensive exhibition for the incentive and sales promotion industry.

A trip to Incentive gives you a first class insight into -

● Sales Incentives and Motivation Schemes
● Premiums and Promotional Merchandise
● Competitions, Awards and Business Gifts
● Brand Loyalty and Awareness Campaigns

In fact, a total range of Sales Promotion products and services essential for every business. You'll always find new ideas, new products being launched, and new services just waiting to be discovered. What's more, you'll find just the right idea to help your business grow, to motivate your staff, to reward dealers and promote your products.

**'INCENTIVE' -
THE PROFESSIONALS CHOICE**

Remember, Incentive is the exhibition supported by the industry's professionals. Incentive is in association with 'Marketing Week' magazine, and endorsed by The Institute of Sales Promotion, the British Promotional Merchandise Association and the Promotional Sourcing Association.

The exhibition is also fully supported by the industry's top magazine 'Incentive Today'.

THE NATIONAL INCENTIVE & PROMOTION EXHIBITION

MAY 12-14 1992, GRAND HALL, OLYMPIA

12 MAY 10AM-6PM   13 MAY 10AM-6PM   14 MAY 10AM-4PM

In Association with **MARKETING WEEK**   and endorsed by   **EPMA** BRITISH PROMOTIONAL MERCHANDISE ASSOCIATION   p   a'   **incentive** TODAY

FREE TICKETS FOR YOU AND YOUR COLLEAGUES

Please clip the coupon below which will bring you free admission to Incentive '92. You'll also receive full details of advance registration which means that you'll be able to avoid any entry formalities on the day of your visit.

Make it a date for Incentive '92, May 12th - 14th 1992, Grand Hall Olympia.

Incentive '92 is organised by Langfords Exhibitions Ltd.
Ridgeland House, 165 Dyke Road, Hove, E. Sussex BN3 1TL. Telephone: (0273) 206722 Fax: (0273) 736250

A Langfords event.

TICKET REQUEST

Please send me _____ tickets for Incentive'92.

Name_____ Position_____

Company_____ Address_____

Postcode_____ Tel. No._____

THE NATIONAL INCENTIVE & PROMOTION EXHIBITION
MAY 12-14 1992, GRAND HALL, OLYMPIA

Return the coupon to: Langfords Exhibitions Ltd., Ridgeland House, 165 Dyke Road, Hove, E. Sussex BN3 1TL.   GA4

Advertising material for event sponsored by trade magazine

reason many venues have specialised in organising consumer events, for which visitors can also be charged an attendance fee.

The competitive strategy of organisers often works against the best interests of exhibitions. Sadly some events are launched to ruin other organisers' events and may run at the same time of year but at a different venue. Others are launched against a much bigger event with a view to being bought out after a year or two.

Another unwelcome motivation is that of publicity for a trade magazine which supports or organises a show in order for it to carry its name. There are numerous examples of this and some work well, especially when the trade magazine dominates its marketplace. On balance however, exhibitors should be cautious. Competing trade magazines are not likely to give free publicity to anything run by a competitor and the failure rate for shows in this sector is very high.

Some experienced exhibitors favour events run by the small independent organisers with only one show in their portfolios. Such organisers often have an in-depth knowledge of the industry, a commitment to it, and the passion to improve, which staff working for the multiple event organisers may lack.

The visitors attending

The buying power and the quantity of visitors to the show will determine its usefulness to most exhibitors. Sadly, most exhibitors assume, often quite wrongly, that the organiser has a special power to attract visitors, and fail to ask pertinent questions regarding the audience.

Some organisers have their events independently audited and can supply a set of figures showing the visitor profiles broken down in a number of ways. This should be encouraged.

Others take the view that the best proof of a show's effectiveness in attracting visitors, especially at trade events, is a list of visitors' names and addresses, supplied to all exhibitors. This practice should also be encouraged. In fact, for small and medium-sized organisations showing in a limited space with a limited staff and budget this second option is to be preferred since it will be difficult with limited means to see every possible prospect during a show. The visitor list will thus be essential if those missed opportunities are to be identified.

Those organisers most unwilling to supply visitor lists – the 'proof of the pudding' – may well have good reason. Commonly, organisers who are also publishers of trade magazines worry that their competitors will mail the list. And the publication of a list means that visitor figures cannot be inflated, which is a common occurrence.

It is the visitors that will make or break a show, and the organiser's ability to attract them should be a major concern. In a difficult economic climate organisers have to spend increasingly large amounts of their budget on attracting exhibitors and consequently have little left with which to attract the visitor. Techniques used may therefore fall into the low-cost category, such as urging exhibitors to mail out invitations, supplying stickers and posters for exhibitor use and swapping exhibition space with trade magazines in exchange for advertising. Such methods are not always beneficial to the exhibitor. Other exhibitors may not mail out the invitations, (many just dump them), the stickers and posters perhaps do more for the organiser's ego than visitor numbers, and advertisements in trade magazines are notoriously ineffective in terms of attracting visitors.

More effective are strong direct mail campaigns and telemarketing programmes using good databases. Also effective, if properly organised, are relevant conferences and seminars, VIP programmes aimed at getting the top buyers to attend, social events aimed at encouraging a longer visit and 'inward missions' of overseas buyers subsidised by the DTI. Exhibitors should also look for signs of a well-conceived public relations campaign highlighting all the *new* products and services to be launched. The reason most visitors go to the show is to see such new products and services.

Paradoxically the reasons the visitors have for going to the event may not be the prime concern of the exhibitor. The first consideration of some exhibitors is that the visitor is simply going to *be there*.

An example of this is the exhibition mounted alongside a conference or seminar, often just a handful of stands. The visitor goes to be a delegate and to hear the sessions but, during the coffee or lunch break, is happy to wander around the stands looking at new commercial developments. Exhibitors may be able to arrange to participate in the conference, to increase their visibility.

Another example is the lateral, but logical thinking of exhibitors who cleverly select shows that are not main-stream events for them but still deliver enough potential buyers to be worth the effort and cost. Some companies selling financial services have found that almost any well-attended trade exhibition presents useful opportunities. Other less obvious examples might be an art-dealer at a swimming pool exhibition (people who can afford swimming pools might also be able to afford art) or a fork-lift truck manufacturer at a frozen food exhibition (supermarkets handling frozen food use fork-lift trucks).

The exhibitors attending

This aspect is nearly always highlighted by organisers selling the fact that an organisation's competitors may already be contracted to attend, and some exhibitors are swayed by the argument, particularly if a large proportion of their competitors will be there. The only logic to this approach is that the promotional activity of those competitors *should* bring in some useful and relevant buyers. If however, they all do nothing in the way of promoting their presence, the benefit is largely lost.

Indeed, as previously stated, some exhibitors have found that being the only organisation in their particular product or service category, has brought considerable business. It is however, a fact that some exhibitors will exhibit to expose themselves and to sell to other exhibitors at the event. Trade magazines find that many of their advertisers are exhibiting and, at some industrial shows, the inter-stand trading between component manufacturers and those selling equipment using the components can be as brisk as that between exhibitors and visitors.

The venue

Exhibitions have been successfully held on boats, trains, in fields and under canvas, as well as in modern purpose-built exhibition halls. And many types of building have been pressed into service for shows including a disused railway station (G Mex in Manchester) and an unwanted car-park (the Barbican exhibition halls in London). An old ice-cream factory in Liverpool was once used for a business to business event and an old agricultural hall of trade in Islington is now the Business Design Centre. Additionally many hotels can hold small to medium-sized events; the Novotel in Hammersmith, the Metropole in Brighton, the Ramada Inn in Fulham, the Hospitality Inn in Glasgow and the Royal Lancaster in West London are all examples.

LONDON HAMMERSMITH

ACCOMMODATION

Each of the 640 comfortable bedrooms offers:

- double bed and single studio bed.
- en suite bathroom with wc, bath, shower and complementary toiletries.
- air conditioning and double glazing.
- spacious desk working area with direct dial telephone.
- radio and remote control colour TV with satellite channels.
- minibar.
- tea and coffee making facilities.
- room service.
- laundry, dry cleaning and shoe shine services.

There are 4 spacious suites, and 4 rooms specially adapted for disabled guests.

CONFERENCES AND MEETINGS

When it comes to organising a meeting or an event, Novotel London offers unrivalled choice of rooms whether for 2 or 900.

Conferences and Banqueting

Novotel London Hammersmith is a true Conference Centre. The Champagne Suite is one of the largest purpose-built venues in the London area. Through thoughtful design it can be adapted to accommodate meetings up to 900. For a format requiring less space the Sommelier suite can accommodate 100 delegates in comfort and style.

Residential Conferences

With 640 rooms - each sleeping at least 2 adults, Novotel London Hammersmith's ability to provide enough rooms to meet your likely needs, and car parking too, is particularly attractive to those organising residential events.

Product Launches

Novotel London Hammersmith is ideally located and equipped for major product launches. The Champagne Suite boasts a sectioned stage which can easily be erected to the required size and shape. Lighting, sound, power, AV, photographic and press facilities are naturally up to full International standards. We can also offer other areas suitable for smaller and specialised launches and promotions.

As part of our service we provide the essential expert advice on staging an event and professional support from planning through to your post-conference press debrief. Our sound and vision rooms act as a nerve centre for the successful stage management of events which are increasingly hi-tech, comforting to know that there are trained operating staff with years of experience and full technical back-up at their fingertips - all at your disposal.

Small Meetings and Training Facilities

Novotel London Hammersmith's strategic position makes it ideal as a meeting centre, for business countrywide as well as delegates to conferences or exhibitions in the hotel. Additional to the Champagne and Sommelier suites, is the Bordeaux suite, comprising smaller purpose-built seminar rooms perfect for board meetings, training or interviews. Each can be set up in the style of your choice with a full complement of AV back up facilities to enhance your presentation. Flexible catering arrangements are available either in a private room or Le Grill. Those on residential courses may also sample the famous Novotel Buffet breakfast to set them up for the day!

EXHIBITIONS

Access and Facilities

Recently completely refurbished our exhibition centre is one of London's most popular and convenient venues for trade and public shows. The exhibition centre is approximately 1300m2 gross with a high floor loading of 110lb sq ft allowing for heavy machinery and stands. For larger shows this space can even be increased to approximately 3370m2 gross with the inclusion of the Sommelier Suite. The exhibition centre has its own access road and loading bays and a visitor's entrance with access points to the other major function suites and the rest of the hotel. Our exhibition team will work with you from the early planning stages right through the event itself to ensure a total success, and we can recommend outside contractors to supply all your ancillary requirements.

LEISURE FACILITIES

Just next to the hotel is the Broadway Squash Club, for squash and weight training. There are a number of health and leisure clubs nearby, also parks and riverside walks. Reception will be pleased to offer information and advice on leisure activities and facilities in the area.

Novotel London Hammersmith
Hammersmith International Centre
1 Shortlands
London W6 8DR
Tel: 081741 1555
Fax: 081 741 2120
Telex: 934539

RESINTER 071 724 1000
Groups: 081 741 3575
Conference Line: 081 741 1888

LOCATION

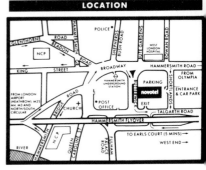

Public Transport

There is easy access to the M4 (London's Heathrow Airport and the M25 are just 20 minutes away), and to the West End just 10 minutes down the road. The hotel has an underground car park with space for 250 cars.

Road and Air Links

Under 5 minutes easy walk from the hotel Hammersmith Underground Station's Piccadilly, Metropolitan and District lines offer fast direct access to Heathrow, Earl's Court, Olympia, the West End and all parts of the Capital. Hammersmith bus and coach station is opposite the rear entrance to the hotel, and the Airbus which runs direct to and from Victoria and Heathrow stops nearby. London cabs are also available day and night.

Olympia and Earl's Court Exhibition centres can be reached in minutes by car, taxi or public transport - they are even close enough to walk.

EXHIBITION CENTRE (Ground Floor)

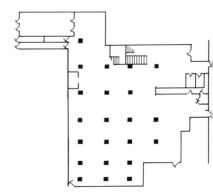

Promotional material for hotel exhibition space

The venue *can* make a difference to the success of an event if visitors find it, or perceive it as, wanting or inconvenient. Alexandra Palace in North London suffers it seems, from a lack of easy access. Many visitors dislike the claustrophobic nature of the low ceilings at the Barbican. The NEC has no social life and too few low-cost hotels nearby for visitors to stay in, a serious criticism for the UK's largest venue.

Certainly, many exhibition halls will need to become more visitor friendly in their approach. Facilities for disabled people although improving, still have a long way to go. Simple things like public telephones mounted at wheelchair height are still comparatively rare. Basic items such as effective air-conditioning are still missing from the most modern London halls, and one refurbished complex, at the time of writing, still had no fire alarm system! The quality of the food supplied by UK exhibition halls and the exploitative prices charged are also the subject of much visitor dissatisfaction and many complaints.

That said, the venue, or perhaps its location, can also seal the success of events. Those in London may benefit from the pull of nearby attractions, the availability of public transport, the attraction for overseas visitors and the huge catchment area of the South East. Those in Harrogate, especially events where visitors might bring their partners for a few days, can benefit from the cosy social ambience and compact nature of the North of England's celebrated spa town as well as the beauty of the nearby countryside. Whilst those in Brighton, Bournemouth, Eastbourne, Torquay or Blackpool may benefit from offering a day or two beside the seaside. The NEC Birmingham is easily accessible by air, rail or road.

Exhibitors should know their customers, and their preferences, in order to evaluate which venues are likely to be popular with them, and therefore visited. Small business exhibitons hoping to attract senior business executives often work better in high quality hotels than in purpose-built halls. Industries where the social side is important might well respond to exhibitions held in Brighton or Harrogate or even, as in the case of one financial event, on an ocean liner.

Timing and frequency

Exhibitors who know their market will be able to judge whether or not the timing of the show is appropriate, in terms of visitors' buying patterns and other possibly competing events which might affect numbers. The weather can have a disastrous affect on visitor numbers, especially if visitors are expected to travel long distances. One organiser of a February event for the UK conference industry has had the event badly hit by blizzards twice in six years. Some events can do very well in a holiday period. The International Exhibitors Association (IEA) in the USA always holds its annual conference and exhibition in August, a ploy which encourages visitors to bring their partners and stay longer, especially those from overseas.

Frequency is another important aspect. Some industries, such as the computer industry, are changing rapidly and new technology is constantly being developed. Two or three events a year might not be too many for some exhibitors in this market. Other industries, such as heavy engineering, have less new technology and may favour an event every two or three years. In Germany, where events are controlled by the venues, direct competition is forbidden and shows are limited to a pre-determined frequency, sometimes only once every five years. Many exhibitors feel that this disciplined approach should be adopted in the UK.

If an event is staged annually it is worth remembering that, on average, 30% of visitors to an exhibition are either new to their company, or new to the industry. This means that those exhibitors not wishing to exhibit at every event, every year could exhibit every three years and meet a completely new audience.

Evaluating the organiser

Event organisers can be trade associations, publishers, venues, local authorities, or private companies. Whatever the category, exhibitors need to ask a number of questions, some of which we have already touched on, in order to better evaluate the organiser and the event:

- Why is the event being staged?
- Who is behind it?
- How long has it been running?
- Is it independently audited?
- Is a visitor list available?

- How will it be promoted to visitors?

- How 'international' is it really?

- What other events does the organiser run?

- Is there a conference/seminars?

- If so, how will the delegates be encouraged to visit the exhibition?

- Is there an entry charge?

- How will visitor quality be maintained on the day?

- What information will visitors have to give?

- Are students being encouraged to attend?

- Can the general public attend?

- Are there any concurrent events running at the venue? What are they?

- Will catalogues be distributed to key buyers in advance of the exhibition?

- What happens to money paid if the event is cancelled or postponed?

Further checks can be made if the event is a regular one. Some exhibitors obtain copies of the last two years' catalogues and check the number of exhibitors that exhibited once but did not return. One business to business show in Buckinghamshire had to replace 80% of its exhibitors, a sure sign that something was badly wrong. Another check can be made by asking to see a copy of the visitor list, or at least a portion of it (to avoid being sent only impressive names, ask for all the names beginning with one letter of the alphabet). Exhibitors can be contacted to ascertain their view of the event. And, perhaps even more relevant, visitors can be contacted to ascertain whether or not they will be going back.

Spotting the potential flop

Experienced exhibitors will often know when a proposed new show is superfluous. The number of events in almost any given industry is, at least in the UK and USA, likely to be more than the industry can support, taking into account the rate of change in technology and audience.

However, shows flop for reasons other than entering a saturated market. The existing economic situation or a war, can have a disastrous effect. The organisers may be inexperienced and the events may be ill-conceived.

There are a number of examples in this last category. Shows featuring retirement options have flopped because potential visitors are already inundated with direct mail compaigns carried out by the financial sector and possibly do not want to be openly admitting their age by going to such an event. A number of similarly ill-thought out attempts have been made to get an event featuring major advertising agencies off the ground when it is known that such companies target their clients on a highly personal basis, and that high spending clients are well aware of the agencies capable of handling their account.

Another area to beware of is the event added to other events on the seemingly logical basis that visitors to one will also be interested enough to visit another. One example of this was an attempt by organisers of a large international gift event for retailers in Sydney to launch a concurrent event featuring other things that gift shop retailers could buy, such as cash registers, point of sale material and security systems. The event flopped because visitors did not have the time to visit the extra event. Another ill-conceived notion was a 'careers fair' organised alonside a UK engineering show, for amongst other things, those looking to change jobs. Understandably, few wanted to be publicly seen to be dissatisfied with their present positions!

There are also some useful pointers to an event's possible demise. The postponement of an event could well be a sign that the show is not selling as quickly as forecast. Similarly industry leaders pulling out or a sharp reduction in the floor-space taken could also be an early warning. Changes in the floor-plan to encompass a press office, an exhibitors lounge, a 'central feature', some seminar rooms, a leaflet distribution point, a trade association lounge or some extra catering areas might also be signs that space is not selling.

Points for Discussion

1 What is the *first* factor in choosing an exhibition?

2 What are the advantages and disadvantages of attending an exhibition sponsored by a trade magazine?

3 Why should organisers supply lists of visitors attending their exhibitions?

4 What might be the advantages of holding an exhibition in a) a hotel in London b) in the NEC c) in Harrogate?

5 What factors influence the timing and frequency of exhibitions?

6 Why might an exhibition flop?

CHAPTER FOUR

MANAGING THE EVENT

Once the die has been cast and an event chosen the next job is to decide on the site, if a choice is allowed (some guidelines on site selection are given in chapter 5). After this the organiser will forward a contract for perusal and signature.

Once the commitment has been legally made there will be many jobs to be done and aspects to consider. Some of these will involve co-ordinating the efforts of more than one individual or department within the organisation and, if there is no full-time exhibition manager (and there generally isn't), then it will be worthwhile appointing someone with the time, and authority, to oversee the project.

Such a manager having been appointed, he or she will need to give consideration to a considerable number of aspects. Some of the main areas are now listed.

The contract

All contracts are subject to UK contract law and, once signed, very hard to change or set aside. Although it will be seen as a tedious and time-consuming job, the exhibition organiser's contract must be read and any terms objected to must be brought to the attention of the organiser for alteration or deletion. Should litigation follow, the courts will assume that the exhibitor was given the opportunity to do this before making the commitment.

Some of the most troublesome clauses will be found in sections relating to what happens if the event is cancelled or abandoned. Clearly, if a company has committed itself to an exhibition which is subsequently cancelled, costs will have been incurred. In some instances a stand will have been designed and possibly purchased for the event. Substantial money may have been committed to advertising and promoting the exhibitor's presence at the show. Special displays and products may have been shipped in and airline tickets and hotel accommodation purchased. Other events may have been turned down in order to partcipate.

A typical organiser's contract will state: 'The exhibitor shall not have any claim against the organiser in respect of any loss or damage consequent upon the failure, for whatever reason, of the exhibition being held.' Such clauses absolve the organiser from any responsibility whatever the loss. Cancellation insurance can be taken out by the exhibitor but such insurance never covers the two most comon reasons for the failure of an event; lack of interest or the insolvency of the organiser. Clearly, from the exhibitors point of view such commitments are serious. Contracts *must* be read.

One organiser's contract held exhibitors liable for any costs to the organiser involved in the postponement or abandonment of the event and even included a clause which allowed the organiser to increase the stand space charges after the contract had been signed. Yet another absolved the organiser from any damage or injury occurring at the show even if caused by the organiser's negligence, and from any loss resulting from incorrect information given by them.

A common complaint of exhibitors is that their stand position has been altered and most contracts allow organisers to do this. One exhibitor, having chosen and paid for a site near a catering area and on a main aisle, found on arrival at the event that the aisle had been closed to form a cul-de-sac and that the catering area had been closed down. A letter to the organiser explaining the reasons for booking a given site would offer some legal protection.

Tied contracts

A cause of many complaints is the 'tied' contract, whereby exhibitors are forced to use one contractor or another to supply stand electrics, flowers, catering requirements, furniture and even photography and audio visual. A study of the prices charged will indicate that they are invariably far higher than any commerical rate charged outside the exhibition hall and this is generally because the hall owner and the organiser have instructed the contractor to elevate their prices to include a commission.

The practice is of course, exploitative and following exhibitor complaints has already led to an investigation by the Office of Fair Trading. Findings were referred to the Monopolies and Mergers Commission which in turn found that a monopoly existed in favour of a number of contractors and in 1990 recommended a number of long overdue changes. At the time of writing these are being implemented.

The Fraud Squad has also investigated the activities of staff working for a major contractor, and a hall manager. The resulting arrests, trial and conviction saw two men sent to prison in 1990 for corruption. Money had been paid to the hall manager for the favour of a lucrative tied contract.

Tied contacts are most commonly applied to the sale of electrical services and catering. There has never been however, any legal testing of the right of either the hall owner or the exhibition organiser to monopolise in this way. Indeed exhibitors who have defied the rules and supplied their own services have been left alone. Those receiving fines have refused to pay them and no action has been taken.

It is taking time for the exhibition industry to reform. Powerful companies such as P & O, which owns Earls Court and Olympia, are fighting to retain their lucrative monpolistic arrangements and their cause is supported by most large exhibition organisers who also make considerable sums of money from the dubious practice. On the other side are the efforts of the National Exhibitors Association (NEA) and others, urging exhibitors to resist, wherever possible, the invidious pressures.

Exhibitors should, in any event, check their contract to ascertain what restrictions exist and, should these appear onerous or unfair, are advised to take the matter up with the organiser. Until January 4 1991 contracts required exhibitors to use only trade union labour but the 'closed shop' is now illegal.

The manual

Having signed the contract, exhibitors will be sent an exhibition manual which will detail the rules of the event, contain helpful information and include order forms for a variety of products and services. These will include: the fascia or name board, the entry required in the catalogue, exhibitor and contractor badges, invitation tickets, stickers and posters, electrical requirements, carpeting, plumbing, compressed air, catering, furniture, photography, floral displays, audio visual and other items. The list seems endless. It is worth however, working methodically through the manual and placing orders for those items required as soon as possible, consistent with payment requirements and company policy on such matters. As indicated above it is also worth remembering that prices charged in the manual may be inflated and exhibitors are advised to check and compare prices with those charged outside.

Furniture can often be bought cheaper than it can be hired, green plants can be bought at garden centres and used in office receptions afterwards and it is often cheaper to hire an electrical socket, even at the high prices charged, and plug in portable spotlights than to allow the hall electrician to supply all the fittings. Catering supplies in particular can be purchased far more cheaply than most tied caterers can supply them. One exhibitor participating in a UK property show needed 10,000 French croissants and was quoted £0.90 each by the organiser's caterer, against the £0.18 each she was able to buy for from an outside baker.

Accommodation

Many organisers appoint an official hotel booking agency for exhibitors to book rooms through, after arranging a commission for themselves. It is therefore worth dealing with the hotels directly, as better rates can often be negotiated. It is also worth considering alternative accommodation to hotel rooms. Most tourist offices maintain lists of first class guest houses, and flats or cottages can often be hired far more cheaply than hotel rooms for those happy with self-catering accommodation. Most exhibitions are held outside the holiday season and the owners of such accommodation are often pleased to be able to let it. Exhibitors have also used boats, caravans and motor-homes to advantage.

Insurance

Exhibitors are required to insure for basic risks such as injury to a third party, or failure to vacate the exhibition hall within the agreed time. Merchandise and equipment can also be insured against theft, a very common occurrence at exhibitions.

At the time of writing there is no insurance protection available for costs incurred as a result of an event which is cancelled or postponed due to lack of support or the insolvency of the organiser. In the event of organiser insolvency the monies paid in advance by exhibitors are nearly always lost – exhibitions are a high-risk business.

Security

Theft is common at exhibition halls, particularly those in London, where insurance companies charge twice the normal premium for loss due to theft.

Exhibitors need to consider seriously the possibilities of theft, and the following pointers will help:

● Build-up and breakdown are the most vulnerable times, when items on the stand, or being loaded onto transport, are left unattended.

● Personal items such as wallets from jackets left over chairs and handbags left lying around, are common targets. A lockable cupboard on the stand helps.

● Other common items stolen are video players, and trollies, particularly at break-down.

● Consider moving all portable valuables from the stand over-night.

● Consider erecting 'night-sheets' to cover the perimeter of the stand.

● Do not pack items in boxes which clearly once held alcoholic drinks.

● Report all theft as soon as possible. A surprisingly high proportion of items taken are hidden in the hall for later collection and are recovered.

● Check the credentials of all contractors arriving to remove items at breakdown. Tractors and outboard engines have been stolen from unsuspecting exhibitors in this way.

- Deliberate espionage does go on at exhibitions. Essential samples have been stolen or damaged and details of leads and orders gained at the event have been removed. Be vigilant.

Administration

A number of basic administrative tasks will need to be addressed. Stand staff will need to be issued with the security passes, car-park passes and exhibitor badges commonly supplied by the organiser. Consideration also needs to be given to some way of recording the identities of visitors. Enquiry pads are sometimes supplied by organisers but, failing this, exhibitors will need to supply their own. Forms to which business cards, (if collected), can be fastened are the most common and will need to accommodate all the information the organisation needs to be able to make best use of the enquiry. Answers to questions relating to when the purchase will be made and who else may be involved in the decision are often vital in building up a complete picture.

Electronics are increasingly used in the on-stand capture of data and one modern system collects information from a bar code printed on a visitor's badge. A 'swipe' reader identifies and stores the information for down-loading later. A simpler version relies on a number printed on a visitor's badge. Exhibitors simply collect numbers and submit a list to the organiser to get a print-out with names and addresses. Despite these improvements many exhibitors still prefer to collect business cards. Others use small pocket-sized tape recorders to good effect.

The non-buying visitors

Many organisations make special provision for the press, putting press-packs in the exhibition press office and having some available on the stand as well.

Fewer make any special arrangements for students. Today's students are, of course, tomorrow's customers and some progressive exhibitors are realising this and distributing simple information sheets with an overview of their particular industry, often provided by the trade association. Others have listed technical problems yet to be solved as 'project work' and some have been pleasantly surprised at the positive response.

The exhibition is however a commercial event and for their part students must realise that exhibitors are predominantly there for commercial reasons – to meet buyers.

Stand staff

According to the Trade Show Bureau in the USA an organisation's top sales performers can be the worst possible choice for exhibition stand work. This still surprises many who regard working on an exhibition stand as essentially a sales activity.

Experienced sales personnel are effective once a visitor has been enticed onto the stand and positively identified as a prospect, or someone who can buy. This activity demands a soft approach rather than a hard-sell, if the visitor is not to be frightened away and it is this temporary change of pace and style that pure sales types find so hard to master.

In fact the techniques are not difficult, but they are different to other forms of selling and there has been a gradual acceptance of the differences in the UK, where an increasing number of organisations are now taking the trouble to train all stand staff in the specialist art of exhibiting.

Some have found that non-sales staff make the best stand staff. Office receptionists, telephonists, secretaries and PA's can be good choices, as can technical staff and those from marketing, advertising and PR. All should be trained. In terms of selection, a broad range of gender, age and race can present the best face to the mixture of visitors who will attend. It should also be remembered that whereas the 'look' of the staff might be deemed important to the image of the stand there is a world of difference between stylish and welcoming, and between attractive and glamorous. Staff should be warm, welcoming, helpful and people-friendly.

A roster of some kind will be needed if staff are always to appear fresh and enthusiastic, and no one person, except perhaps the stand manager, should have to work a whole day. Exhibition stand duty is very tiring, both physically and emotionally and 'two hours on, one hour off' is an ideal to strive for, with no one working more than four hours. Some organisations, faced with a working exhibition day running from 10.00 am till 7.00 pm would run three shifts. Tired staff will be a liability rather than an asset, and it should be noted that an afternoon shift is more tiring than a morning one, due to natural bodily rhythms.

A good stand manager will lay down strict rules for 'housekeeping' and 'timekeeping' and will not allow staff to eat, drink, smoke or to sit down, (unless for good reason) whilst on the stand. Procedures will also be worked out whereby staff away from the stand but still in the exhibition, can be contacted (usually by pager) should a visitor request to see them. Alternatively, the stand manager should know what time they will be back.

A proper 'de-briefing' session as soon as the show is over each day will ensure that vital information collected but not recorded in the heat of the moment is not lost and that any operational problems emerging in the course of running of the stand can be dealt with.

Follow up

For many exhibitors the real work comes after the exhibition, when the leads are followed up. Some exhibitors will have a planned approach, telephoning suitable prospects identified at the exhibition and inviting them to an open day, factory tour, seminar or road-show. Others will mail an offer of a free gift if an order is placed. Sadly, many others will fail to even send requested literature.

Conventional wisdom says that all exhibition leads should be followed up within two weeks of the exhibition. Certainly those who specifically requested a contact should be followed up much faster. Some kind of priority ranking on the original enquiry forms would be helpful in identifying the most urgent calls to make.

Despite conventional wisdom, some exhibitors are finding that, since some buyers will be inundated with follow-up letters just after a show, a letter a month later to those who simply collected information is most effective.

Points for Discussion

1 What sort of questions should an exhibitor ask as he or she reads the organiser's contract?

2 What are the two most common causes of an event being cancelled?

3 How can security on the stand be achieved. What are the two most vulnerable times?

4 Why do exhibition organisers encourage the press to attend? Why should they be concerned whether students attend?

5 Describe someone who would make an ideal member of the stand staff.

6 What is the optimum follow-up time for leads after an exhibition?

7 As an exhibitor, what reforms would you press for in the exhibition industry? As a hall-owner, or organiser, would you resist these?

CHAPTER FIVE

THE

STAND: BASIC

CONSIDERATIONS

Important decisions involve the size, shape and location of the stand as well as the strategy and tactics of stand design. Whether or not the event is used for a hard-sell or for entertaining are major considerations.

In many of these areas a good exhibition stand designer can greatly assist the exhibitor and some are now closer to being overall exhibition consultants rather than simply designers, ('marketing-led' rather than 'design-led').

It is important to look at the stand from a marketing perspective, that is, to look at what works, not necessarily what looks impressive. And to get a stand that really works there are some marketing decisions that only the exhibitor can really make.

Size of stand

A number of factors commonly affect the size of stand chosen. These include: budget constraints, the size of item(s) to be exhibited, the need for seated discussions and on-stand hospitality, the company's position in the marketplace, the perceived need to show 'strength', corporate ego and the size of a major competitors presence. The need to provide conference areas and space for demonstrations will also have an important bearing on the size of the stand (see section on confering on the stand later in chapter).

However, the size of the stand should be related to the main reason for being at an exhibition – to hold conversations with potential customers. And the more potential customers that can be seen in the time available, the more successful the show will be. This rightly shifts the emphasis firmly towards the main function of the stand as a temporary sales showroom and one in which the optimum numbers of sales staff can comfortably operate to converse with all the potential customers that an exhibition delivers.

A calculation, therefore, of the optimum staff numbers and the space required will be a vital check on objectives, even if the space figure reached is unaffordable and sights have to be lowered.

As an example, the exhibitor may decide that from a total of 5,000 visitors to a three day event only 600 are likely to be potential buyers (this figure will vary considerably from organisation to organisation). For the exhibitor's particular product or service let us say a total of ten minutes conversation is, in this instance, deemed appropriate, (it should rarely be much longer). This means that each salesperson can process around five potential clients per hour, allowing for wasted time such as breaks. In an eight hour day this gives around 40 contacts per salesperson, or 120 over the three days. To handle 600 potential customers in this way will need five salespeople.

Each salesperson will need a minimum of four square metres of clear floor-space, to allow for their own requirements and that of their potential customer and a stand providing this will need to provide a minimum clear floor area of twenty square metres, not allowing for displays, storage areas, bar areas, conferring areas or space for non-sales staff.

Note from the above calculations a reduction in the time spent with each potential client from ten to five minutes, (which is certainly attainable with training), will dramatically reduce the space required and hence the budget needed. Also note that any percentage of the 600 potential customers may be aimed for, with corresponding reductions in space and cost, an approach that, for most, will be appropriate.

Shape of stand

Any retailer knows that the shop 'frontage' (the length of the window area exposed to shoppers walking outside), is what pulls people in and the

Various kinds of stand frontage

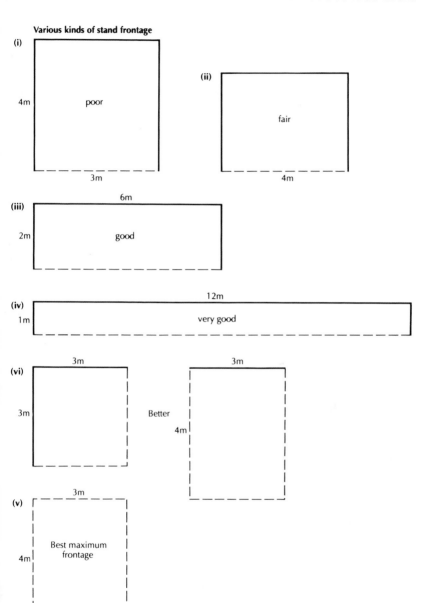

longer the frontage, the better the pull. Exhibition stands are similar in function in that they have to attract and stop a moving target and thus the frontage is a vital consideration.

It follows then, that if the stand size is to be say twelve square metres there are a number of ways this can be bought. A three metre frontage and a four metre depth will not work as well as a four metre frontage and a three metre depth. However a six metre frontage with a two metre depth, (if sufficient), works best of all. Indeed some experienced exhibitors with only flat graphics to display are starting to request one metre depths. Since space is sold in the UK (though not in the USA) by the square metre, a twelve by one metre area will cost the same as a four by three metre stand.

Obviously total frontage can be increased by picking a corner site with two open sides, an end of 'block' position with three open sides or an 'island' position with four open sides.

As a guide an average walking speed at an exhibition is approximately one metre per second.

Location of stand

Despite the claims of many organisers anxious to sell *all* their spaces, the location of the stand can make a difference to the individual exhibitor. In a recent survey carried out by the National Exhibitors Association (NEA) stand location was identified as one of the top three factors affecting success (the other two were stand design and staff training).

Assuming the exhibitor can book early and has a free choice there are a number of worthwhile considerations:

● A visit to the exhibition hall, whilst another show is in progress, can pay dividends. Traffic flow can be identified, as can 'dead' areas. In the UK these will include a number of 'cul-de-sac' sites away from main gangways in the Barbican Exhibition Centre, London, the Avon room at Wembley and Hall 8 in the Brighton Metropole complex. In one of the Melbourne centres in Australia, a giant floor to ceiling window in one section allows sunlight to blind visitors. Areas other than the main hall are often added by organisers if demand is higher than anticipated and are frequently ignored by busy visitors.

Various kinds of stand frontage

i) Run of block

ii) Corner

iii) End of block

iv) Island

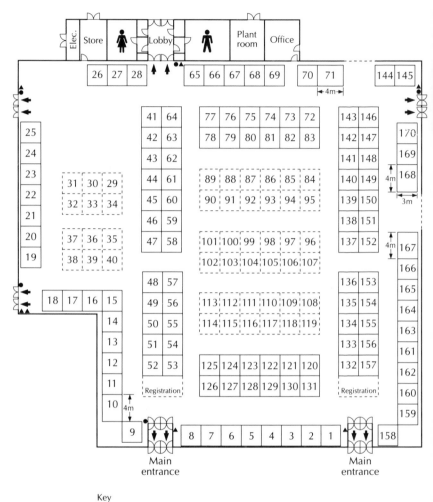

Key

 Male toilets

 Female toilets

▲ Fire extinguisher

● Fire bell

◄ Fire exit

Plan of a typical exhibition hall

• In a large show, stands that visitors would reach at the end of a day will often be missed as visitors get tired and head for home. In this respect, upstairs galleries can be a poor choice. With regard to large shows in the UK remember that UK hotel prices do not encourage visitors to stay overnight. In the USA and in the rest of Europe, each visitor averages two days per event, as comparatively, hotel prices are much cheaper. In the UK anything that cannot be seen in a day trip (average four to five hours at the event) probably won't be seen at all. Large events at the NEC, Birmingham are especially prone to this late afternoon exodus with whole halls sometimes ignored.

• A stand around the perimeter of the event can often be a good choice. Traffic flow, due to the presence of bars, food areas, toilets and information points is often greatest there and exhibitors, for the disorientated visitor, are easy to find and return to.

• Stands too close to bar and food areas can suffer from the overspill if these get busy. Drinkers and eaters are not necessarily potential customers.

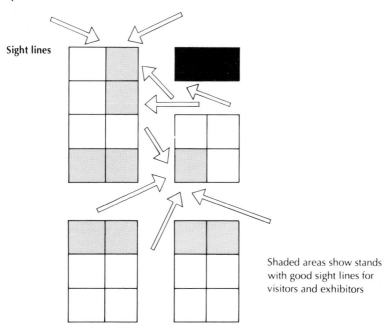

Sight lines

Shaded areas show stands with good sight lines for visitors and exhibitors

● Many experienced exhibitors avoid stands opposite an entrance, on the basis that visitors walk right by them to get into the main body of the show.

● Some experienced exhibitors consistently book a stand near to toilets since it is one place that almost everyone visits. One exhibitor selling exclusively male products, always books a stand next to the ladies toilet, to make contact with men waiting outside for their partners.

● Some stands have better visibility than others, those facing the ends of aisles or at the bottom of stairs, for example. Check these 'sight lines' on the floor plan (see the diagram on p. 45).

● Seminars and other such events arranged by the organiser can draw useful traffic, as long as they are successful, and a site near the area where these are happening can be an excellent choice.

● A company's major competitor(s) at the show will draw many potential customers. Some experienced exhibitors, recognising this, pick sites close to their largest competitors and benefit.

● Other exhibitors may be selling items which are complementary to your own. If your product is cookery books, for example, a stand next to an oven manufacturer could be an excellent choice.

● Activities of other exhibitors can hurt your own efforts. Would you want to be opposite one operating a robot, using loud music, or giving away gallons of free wine? Check with the organiser.

● There is no law to say that exhibitors may only buy one stand. If budget and staffing permits, two or three smaller stands may be preferable to one large stand, especially if they are spread out across a larger event. This strategy is particularly suitable for companies with ranges of different products.

● Two stands straddling an aisle can be used most effectively (see p. 45).

Shell schemes

Exhibitors are commonly offered floor space to erect their own displays, or a 'shell scheme' consisting of already erected walls within which displays

Typical shell scheme

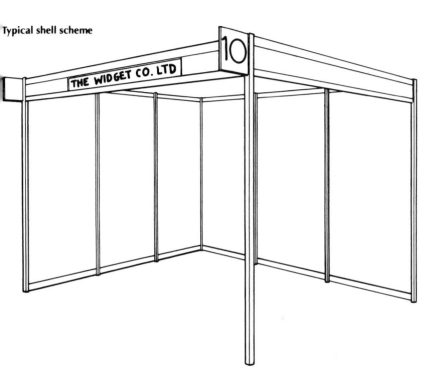

can be built. Modern shell schemes are built up from panels which may be loop-nylon finish or similar, in order to accept Velcro fixings which enable flat, light items such as posters, photographs, signs and pre-cut or pre-formed letters to be easily and quickly applied, and removed without damage.

Another trend is towards a 'package deal' which can include a power point, basic lighting and basic furniture. These can be very attractive to the small exhibitor on a budget, since the organiser will be buying in bulk and therefore at a lower price than the items could be supplied individually. Shell schemes vary in price but the difference is normally around £20 more per square metre than floor-space, giving an extra cost of £120 on a basic three metre by two metre stand.

Conferring on the stand

An early decision is required on whether a seated area for discussions with customers and potential customers is needed. If conversations are only going to be a few minutes duration with the objective being to collect a lead and move quickly on to the next visitor, then a seated area will be superfluous. In this instance sales staff can use public facilities for those few visitors needing a little more time. Some progressive organisers of exhibitions provide special exhibitor lounges where such meetings can take place.

For some exhibitors, a conference area, perhaps doubling as a stand office, will be essential. However, the provision should hinge around the needs of the visitor, not the comfort of stand staff.

Entertaining at exhibitions

In terms of meeting objectives at exhibitions, entertaining, or 'corporate hospitality' is often misused. It can be a highly effective way of consolidating business, of supporting the exhibition stand or even as an alternative to exhibiting.

1 *On-stand hospitality*   is virtually non-existent in the USA, because of exhibition hall rules on drinks and food at stands, but it is almost mandatory at some shows in mainland Europe. The question of on-stand hospitality needs careful reflection. In most cases it simply will not be necessary to provide anything for visitors since the majority will often only be staying for a few minutes.

Tea, coffee or more commonly now, cold soft drinks, such as fruit juices, are as far as most exhibitors go and with good reason, since these are most acceptable to the majority of visitors. Alcoholic drinks, once the centrepiece of many exhibition stands, are very expensive and the highest costs are possibly the hidden ones. A bar takes up expensive stand space and needs staff to run it and keep it clean and tidy. The free drink can attract the wrong type of visitor and the party atmosphere can actually alienate and repel some serious buyers, who may not be able to physically get onto the stand over the busy lunchtime period. Sales staff can quickly become guests and spend time drinking instead of looking for prospects. After a midday drink their performance is likely to diminish.

Ideally a bar area, if provided, should be discreet and 'invitation only', and sales staff should be actively discouraged from indulging.

Better ways of organising on-stand entertaining are in the simple provision of nibbles (crisps, canapes, raw vegetable dips) and soft drinks. Fruit juices in cartons with attached straws can be economically stacked in a fridge and there is no washing up. In Australia a common sight is a drink chiller full of colourful fruit juice and disposable cups sometimes printed with the company name. The slowly turning rotisserie attracts attention too. Other alternatives seen are mineral water dispensers and hot chocolate machines (a hot drink could be a useful way to retain visitors on the stand, should you wish to do so).

Even those exhibitors attending events where alcoholic hospitality is the accepted thing can beat the system to their own advantage. One manufacturer of animal foods, participating in UK agricultural shows, was aware that his competitors were running the beer tents popular with farmers. Rather than compete directly he arranged for supplies of strong hot coffee to be served from 2.00 pm onwards so that customers could sober up a little before going home.

On a more serious note, although a number of people drinking and driving has thankfully dropped, there is growing concern that a visitor to an exhibition, if irresponsibly given too much to drink by an exhibitor, could sue for damages if the drunkeness led to an accident. The caveat also applies to our next section.

2 *Off-stand hospitality* in a nearby hospitality 'suite' can solve a lot of the problems associated with on-stand entertaining mentioned above. Not only can pre-selected clients and potential clients be invited but any new potential client identified on the stand can also attend. The trend however, is to run demonstrations, short seminars or give opportunities for hands-on trials in the suite, rather than just entertain. In this way the best use of company resources and opportunities at the show can be made by having the suite working in conjunction with the stand. The suite, if hired, may also be used for other activities such as

press briefings, sales training and as an office HQ for the event.

An additional dimension with hospitality is to run an event outside show hours thus making the best use of staff time during the show. A dinner or breakfast is an excellent way of saying thank you to existing clients and unlike lunch during show hours, doesn't tie up valuable staff during the busiest period on the stand when lots of potential customers could be passing. One trend is for these events to take the form of a business presentation coupled with entertaining, perhaps run as a special breakfast on the first morning of the show and a 'sneak preview' of new products and services displayed.

Some companies use the occasion of the show to forge social links by organising theatre or concert visits or sporting events. Inviting top customers for a day's golf or a day at the races before or after an event and, paying for their accommodation, could in some circumstances, be appropriate.

3 *Entertaining as an alternative* to taking a stand is a highly cost-effective way of doing business. Some exhibitors have found that simply booking into a nearby hotel and running a hospitality suite and even a mini exhibit without attending the show at all can work very well. The potential customers are 'in town' and if they can be enticed to visit, should be in a buying mood. Naturally this approach only delivers those visitors who can be identified before the event, although this may well be enough for many companies. Smaller hotels, particularly those with a good food reputation, are often an excellent choice for the exhibitor wishing to pursue this strategy.

Points for Discussion

1 In what ways do being 'market-led', rather than 'design-led' affect exhibtion stands?

2 Draw up a plan of an exhibition hall showing good and bad sites.

3 Why is the stand frontage so important?

4 Why might an exhibitor need a seated conference area on the stand?

5 What are the problems associated with offering alcoholic drinks on stands?

CHAPTER SIX

STAND DESIGN STRATEGY

In order to make the most of all the opportunities presented by visitors passing the stand, some way of getting them to stop has to be found. Very few visitors will walk onto a stand for no particular reason and, unless they have heard or read about what is being offered and are already interested, a way must be found very quickly is catch their attention and spark their interest.

Good stand staff can do this essential 'trawling' by skilfully approaching as many visitors as possible with carefully worded questions and it can be argued that this is the best and cheapest option especially for the smaller exhibitor. Indeed, an increasing number of larger companies are finding out just how effective at attention-grabbing their own trained staff can be (see chapter 8).

Catching attention and sparking interest however, can also be effectively done by a well thought-out, though not necessarily expensive stand design, and it is worth looking at some of the fundamental considerations.

Focus

It goes without saying, but is not always heeded, that the products (or services) being offered should really be the stars of the show. More specifically it is the benefits of buying them that should clearly and quickly come across to passing visitors if the maximum number are to be attracted. Much unnecessary effort is invested by exhibitors in presenting their logos,

Hodder & Stoughton's stand at the Frankfurt Book Fair

but the objective must be to win customers, not Arts Council awards, and corporate identity programmes are better aimed at shareholders than buyers. Visitors to exhibitions are really only interested in ways that they can do their job better or cheaper and everything on the stand should be geared to conveying this message as quickly and effectively as possible.

Content of the stand

According to research into visitors motivations for visiting an exhibiton over half (54%) do so to look for new products, new services and new ideas. The key word is *new* and a stand featuring the new, and proclaiming the fact loudly and clearly will always attract more serious visitors than more subtle neighbours.

It follows from this that some ruthless pruning of what is shown on the stand could pay dividends. Recognising the limitations of what can actually be accomplished at an exhibition has benefited many exhibitors. By featuring new lines an exhibitor can maximise the number of contacts made and then sell in depth after the show (it's far cheaper too). Products and services that can easily be dramatised are also a good choice for the same reason.

The message

Given the amount of time visitors have (about five hours for most UK events) and the few seconds it takes to walk past a stand, simplicity makes sense, and this can mean distilling the sales message down to one clear proposition. Despite the emphasis understandably placed by stand designers on expensive pictures, simple words can often work better to attract interest and even pre-select prospects. Good headline writers are not much in evidence at shows but should be. Some examples of exhibition stand 'headlines' follow.

- A company handling overseas freight simply stated: **'Ten new ways to save money'** and had the ten ways printed on a leaflet which was exchanged for a business card.

- A manufacturer of space heaters for garage workshops, which burned waste oil removed from customers' cars proclaimed: **'Free heat from waste oil'**.

● A financial company only interested in investors visiting a 'money' show with £500,000 or more to invest used the simple instruction: **'Stop here only if you've got half a million or more'.**

● A computer software company offering advanced programmes with endless possibilities used a slowly turning three inch diameter world globe with the headline: **'A whole world of applications'.**

● Humour played a part in a Sydney based tour operator's headline which encapsulated the possibilities available for those wanting to holiday in Australia: **'There's more to Australia than bloody crocodiles'**, a slogan which stopped everyone with a smile.

Remember that the objective of the design is to stop visitors and spark initial interest. Selling in depth comes later, perhaps even after the show. Headlines also benefit from the use of proven key words. As well as *new* and *free*, the words *now*, *here*, *win*, *you*, *your*, *stop*, can all be usefully employed.

For many exhibitors, particularly on small stands, an effective stand design can depend upon a good headline.

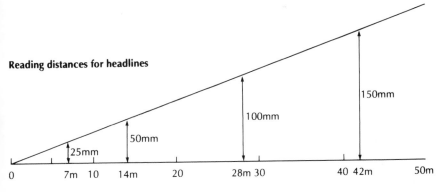

Reading distances for headlines

	DISTANCE	CAP HEIGHT	PANEL DEPTH
UP TO	7m	25mm	45mm
"	14m	50mm	90mm
"	28m	100mm	180mm
"	42m	150mm	270mm
"	84m	300mm	−
"	110m	400mm	−

But whatever form of words are selected the acid-test of a stand headline, and arguably the whole design, is that it should convey a benefit that is obvious to passing visitors and which can be absorbed in a few seconds. Generally visitors should not have to wonder what it is that is being sold. Headlines should therefore be rendered in as large a typeface as is practicable, (see the diagram on p. 55).

Staff as design

Many exhibitors, and some stand designers, fail to realise that the staff themselves, particularly on a small stand, can provide the majority of the visual impact. An all-white stand with staff in bright red jackets can look stunningly effective for little cost and exhibitors dressing staff in this way have noted how it focuses visitor attention on them. Uniforms, and a uniform-look can convey a message (staff for a sales training company dressed in battle fatigues) or, a sense of occasion, (white tuxedos and bow ties). Some exhibitors find that, even when walking around the show or taking a refreshment break, staff dressed for the occasion continue to promote their product or service to visitors.

Visitor psychology

An 'open' stand is generally accepted as the best approach. Anything on the perimeter or frontage of the stand can act as an undesirable barrier between exhibitor and visitor. For this reason many experienced exhibitors avoid putting desks, flowers, fences or anything similar on the frontage of the stand which might physically discourage visitors. For the same reason exhibitors avoid putting the stand up on a platform and even match their carpet to that in the aisles.

The skills of a good stand designer will be brought into play when such aspects as colours, shapes, surfaces, angles, materials and typefaces are all considered. Combinations of these can suggest hi-tech, honesty, friendliness, efficiency, exclusivity and value for money, as can the furniture and other accessories and decorations used.

Themed stands are a good way to attract attention and increase memorabilty although it is a common occurrence for visitors to remember the theme and forget the product, or the organisation. An aura of

A themed stand

exclusivity can be achieved by breaking all the rules and closing off the stand to all but invited guests.

An exhibition is an experience that can, unlike most other media, play on all senses. Effective use can therefore be made of sound, in terms of music, or just a machine working. Smells can also work for the exhibitor and the enticing aroma of cooking food can act as a magnet, as can the taste. Some exhibitors are using ionisers to create a stimulating, fresh atmosphere.

On-stand promotion

The special nature of exhibitions, where buyers are met face-to-face gives an opportunity for demonstrations to attract attention and build interest. These can be very simple. A carpet cleaner was demonstrated by giving away small samples of soiled carpet and the cleaner and letting visitors try it for themselves, always good psychology. A more theatrical, but no less impressive and effective approach was taken by a manufacturer of glue used to bond roofing felt. Pieces of felt were glued together and visitors were invited to try to pull them apart. A jig was designed and set up for the purpose with a large dial showing how strong a pull the visitor was exerting.

Some exhibitors buy in professional help for their event; entertainers and fire-eaters, sword-swallowers, jugglers, unicyclists, robotic dancers, stilt-walkers, acrobats and robots have all been used. Possibly most popular are magicians using tricks which use the product, or highlight some feature of it. One magician at a travel show staged a trick where visitors were given the chance to participate and win a free weekend in a hotel but only if they parted with one of their business cards in exchange for a playing card. A magician at a financial show used a rod with ascending and descending pom-poms to illustrate the ups and downs of the economy.

Competitions can be effective if they build traffic, encourage participation or provide a conversation opener. One UK printer provides a golf putting-green area on the stand and a chance to sink a putt and win a prize. The American company manufacturing the Frisbee flying discs utilises a competition where the disc has to be skimmed through a hole in a target. One exhibition company invites visitors to take a baseball and pitch it against a computer target which records the speed on impact. The idea selected doesn't have to have a direct link with the product but it helps if it does.

The Polaroid company invited visitors at a recent year event to try to 'catch' the image printed on a spinning wheel by using a Polaroid camera. Visitors' efforts were developed in a few minutes and prizes instantly awarded to successful participants. Other promotional gimmicks used include a draw for prizes using visitors' business cards, quizzes, and estimating how many items in a jar. At a financial event, visitors were asked to estimate the Financial Times Stock Market Index on a given day after the show. Ironically the day chosen was the infamous 'Black Monday', when the market collapsed!

Some on-stand promotions are based on distributing something to potential buyers prior to the show, or as they enter the show, to encourage them to come to the stand. Lucky numbers, where the number issued is matched with those published on the stand to win a prize is the simplest device. Invisible ink can be printed onto mailing pieces to describe prizes to be won, with the essential developing pens in the hands of the stand sales team. Bar codes and 'swipe' readers can serve a similar function. And jigsaw puzzle pieces can be distributed with an invitation to call on the stand and 'complete the picture'. Keys can be mailed out, which may, or may not open a box containing a prize. The possibilities are endless. If there is a caveat to promotion on the stand it is that care must be taken to ensure that the gimmick does not detract from the main purpose – to talk business.

Literature

Brochures spread out on tables often don't get taken at all and soon get things spilt on them. Literature racks, and leaflet dispensers, either wall-mounted or free-standing, provide a way of displaying literature without tables taking up valuable space. Inexpensive leaflets can be located at the front of the stand for visitors to help themselves. Expensive literature, and that which exhibitors wish to restrict, should only be given out once a customer or potential customer has been identified. In the USA it is common practice for exhibitors to hand out their literature only in exchange for business cards.

Furnishing and accessories

A wide range of stand furnishings are offered to exhibitors by companies specialising in the hire of such items. For most exhibitors the basics are:

● **A lockable cupboard** in which to store literature and personal effects. The tall versions can also provide a useful writing and work surface area.

● **Chairs to sit on** are often misused by staff looking to rest rather than being offered to visitors. Some exhibitors are discovering the psychological benefits of high bar stools from which sales staff can talk to visitors whilst seated, without seeming rude.

● **Flowers** can give a stand a welcoming look and a homely, environmentally friendly feel. Reds and yellows are especially welcoming. Green plants such as weeping figs, rubber plants and swiss-cheese plants can also be used to good effect, as long as they are not used to block the front of the stand. The 'one metre rule' for stand design indicates that nothing is read if placed below one metre from the floor and troughs of flowers can be usefully employed to fill these areas.

● **Lighting** may simply take the form, on a small three metre by two metre stand, of a five foot florescent tube and/or two 150 watt spotlights. Good lighting can attract the visitor's eye and poor lighting can ruin a good display. Care may need to be taken with the use of too many hot spotlights in a small area, and consideration may need to be given to the effect of types of light on different colours. Lighting hired at exhibitions is expensive and exhibitors are advised to check and cost their requirements. Most find that bringing their own system is far cheaper than asking the exhibition hall contractors to do the work.

Audio-visual

The growth of low-cost VHS video systems has put such tools within the budget of most exhibitors. A video player and monitor is easy and relatively cheap to hire and can be a low-cost way to attract some attention as well as convey information. Sadly the imagination of most exhibitors seems to begin and end with the corporate video, often a poor choice for exhibition stand use.

Information conveyed by video can be on a continuous tape and activated by the stand staff when required. It should show some aspect of the product which is otherwise hard to describe and doesn't need a sound-track since the staff can supply the voice-over, in any language needed.

Any video that attracts attention will do. One company, exhibiting in Russia gathered crowds around the stand by playing music videos of 60s hits. British Petroleum (BP) used vintage footage of bygone motor races to attract visitors. Others simply used their TV monitor to broadcast news and sports events to stop passing visitors. Dozens of TV monitors can also be stacked into video-walls for maximum impact, by those with large budgets.

Another common on-stand use of audio-visual is the slide programme projected onto a suitable surface supplied by most exhibition panel manufacturers.

The do-it-yourself approach

None of these ideas are particularly difficult to understand and hundreds of thousands of stands are effectively thought out without the help of a professional stand designer or the employment of a contractor. There are now dozens of simple modular panel systems on the market which can be transported in a car boot and assembled and erected in minutes.

A list of suppliers of such systems is given in Appendix 6 at the back of this book and for the majority of exhibitors the purchase of these will open the door to low-cost exhibiting. As a guide, only exhibitors spending £10,000 or more on participating will find a stand designer and/or contractor necessary.

The following is a list of criteria which might be considered when designing a stand, or briefing a designer:

- To be easy, quick and low-cost to build.
- To be reusable at other events.
- To be light to transport.
- To be easy and quick to erect and dismantle on site.
- To be visually pleasing.
- To attract visitors.
- To reflect the corporate identity.

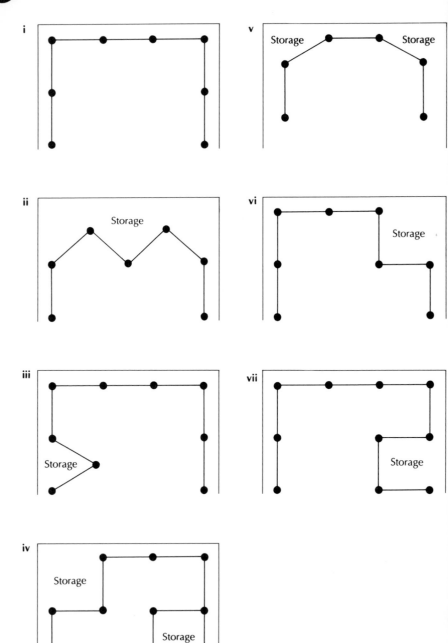

Various formats for inside a shell scheme

Stand layout

i) Poor

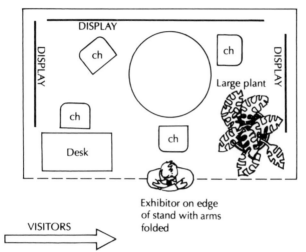

Exhibitor on edge
of stand with arms
folded

ii) Good

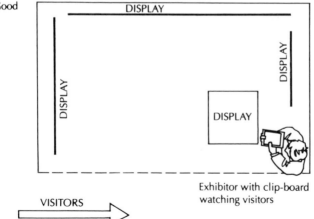

Exhibitor with clip-board
watching visitors

- To comply with the rules of the exhibition, i.e. the height restriction, weight etc.

- To comply with safety and fire regulations.

- To allow free movement of visitors onto the stand.

- To showcase staff and/or products.

- To be visible from as far away as possible.

- To position us as the biggest, friendliest, most high-tech, most exclusive, most environmentally-friendly, etc.

- To provide a conference/seating facility.

- To provide a hospitality facility.

- To provide lockable storage for brochures, equipment and personal effects.

- To provide a wall area for displaying photos and posters.

- To provide a means of distributing company literature.

- To provide a facility for showing videos, slides and film.

- To be well lit.

- To be easy to keep clean.

Points for Discussion

Imagine your college took a stand at an exhibition aimed at fourteen to sixteen year olds with the intention of telling them about options at sixteen in your local area.

1 What slogan would you use to attract attention?

2 Design posters, a brochure and leaflets that could be made available on the stand. Remember, literature distributed freely to the public must be kept cheap to produce.

3 Produce story-boards for a video marketing your college.

4 Find out from suppliers how much it might cost to build your stand and how much it might cost to run it for three days.

CHAPTER SEVEN

EXHIBITION

PUBLICITY

There are two schools of thought on the subject of exhibition publicity. Some exhibitors, particularly the smaller participants, do not publicise their presence at the event. They believe that the organiser's promotion will bring sufficient numbers of interested visitors to the show and past the stand.

This approach is valid in the case of consumer events. It is also valid for many small organisations at trade exhibitions, especially those attracting an international audience. It is worthwhile simply taking a small space and recovering the cost of the modest investment by diligently stopping passing visitors and 'prospecting' (see chapter 8).

Those exhibitors with a larger financial commitment will want to capitalise on their investment by publicising their presence and the products or services they offer to as wide an audience as possible, thereby maximising the number of potential buyers visiting the stand. Such exhibitors will allocate substantial sums to advertising, promotion and public relations activities thereby helping the organiser, as well as other exhibitors.

The organiser's promotional efforts will be aimed at a very general audience, with a view to attracting thousands of them to visit the event. The exhibitors' efforts will generally be directed at a far smaller audience, the hundreds or possibly far smaller numbers of potential clients with a specific interest in buying the product or service they are displaying. Indeed, in many industries, the conversion of only one or two 'possibles' to prime prospects likely to buy may be enough to fully justify the expenditure incurred at the show. It is worth a little effort to ensure that such potential buyers are identified before the exhibition and given every encouragement to attend and visit the stand.

There are those exhibitors who feel that their expenditure on publicity is simply bringing in buyers for their competitors to meet and for the larger exhibitors this is certainly the case. However, buyers always want to approach a number of sources of supply before making a decision and will attend an exhibition with this in mind. Most of the key purchasers in an industry get invitations from a large number of suppliers as well as being exposed to the organiser's publicity and it is very rare for one message or exhortation to be wholly responsible for the visit. Given this, the best approach for the individual exhibitor would seem to be to assume that the key buyers will be attending anyway and to ensure that the visit includes some time at their own stand.

Those that want the buyers' undivided attention can accomplish this before or after the event (or even in some cases, during the event) with factory visits, private exhibitions, roadshows, seminars and corporate hospitality.

Many of the most effective ways of bringing visitor traffic to the stand are low-cost and can be used to good effect by the smallest of exhibitors. This being the case, an appreciation of all the techniques will be useful to everyone.

Publicity and the sales force

The best potential clients may be known to the sales force or can be identified from sources such as good mailing lists, directories and lists of members of professional bodies. It is sensible to contact these clients and invite them to visit the stand, preferably by appointment. Specific reasons need to be given, such as the launch or improvement of a new product or service, or special discounts on prices applying for the period of the show. The number of top quality visitors to the stand can be dramatically increased in this way at minimum cost. Invitations can be sent by mail but will be far more effective if backed up by telephone or by a personal call.

There is a subsidiary benefit to this activity and to much other publicity. Even potential customers who do not attend are reminded that the exhibitor is still active in the market.

Should a high response to this very personal approach be noted it may be necessary and worthwhile to consider the work load of stand staff. If all the opportunities are to be taken advantage of, time has to be found to talk to the passing visitors.

Organisers will often supply invitation tickets free of charge. This is not a charitable act since the organisers want them distributed by exhibitors, whose efforts will account for at least 50% of the visitors attending a trade event. The tickets will give basic details about the show dates, times, venue, travelling to the venue and car-parking. The location of the exhibitor's stand within the show may need to be added by the exhibitor.

Direct Mail

Organisers will usually distribute a substantial number of invitation tickets through magazine inserts and direct mail. However, remember that exhibitor activity in this respect should be focused towards those potential customers identified as specifically interested in the exhibitor's products or services.

For some exhibitors however, a broader direct mail campaign would be a useful addition to exhibiting. A common method is simply to mail invitations out with invoices and statements, in order to attract and encourage customers to visit the stand.

Some companies have built up substantial and valuable lists of potential customers at considerable cost to themselves and some organisers buy sets of name and address labels from such exhibitors, or pay for a mail-shot. This occurs when the exhibiting organisation's information is better than that obtainable by the organiser, and is most likely to occur at vertical (specialised) exhibitions.

On the other hand, the organiser may have a very valuable list of visitors who attended the previous event and exhibitors may be able to mail such a list to potential customers. Some organisers will supply a complete set of name and address labels free of charge, taking the sensible view that the cost, (approx. £20 per 1,000), is small compared to the mailing cost (from £250 per 1,000) and the benefits obtained. These include an increased awareness of the event and more visitors enticed to attend as a result of the exhibitor's mailing.

An example of an exhibition magazine insert

Even at a small charge, such a list would be well worth having. Whether supplied as labels or a simple listing, the exhibitor can select the small proportion he/she wishes to target. Many organisers' lists can now be broken down and supplied by company type, size, geographical area and the job title of the visitor. As with all mailing lists the information is the property of the owner and exhibitors should enquire about any legally enforceable restrictions on copying the list for multiple mailings or transferring names to a permanent database.

As with all direct mail, the list and the actual offer made to the recipients form the two most important factors affecting response. Exhibitors have also used a range of creative devices to dramatise and highlight their offers. 'Teaser' mailing campaigns have effectively aroused curiosity and one exhibitor won the hearts of many potentially footsore visitors by mailing out, a few days before the show, a pair of cushioned insoles designed to relieve aching feet.

The catalogue

Most organisers generate a catalogue of exhibitors which is given away, or sold to visitors. Some organisers even mail key buyers the catalogue before the show, so that they can plan their visits to exhibitors of special interest. A modern trend is for catalogues to be printed in full in magazines distributed prior to the show. The thinking here is that even those who don't attend will have the exhibitors' details and others may be encouraged to make a visit once the exhibitors' names, and details of their products and services, are known. Some exhibitors feel that this method cuts down the number of visitors actually attending the event, who might have come if only to pick up a catalogue.

The catalogue entry is one of the most neglected areas of low-cost publicity and bearing in mind the length of time some catalogues may be kept, exhibitors should put as much care into the writing of their catalogue entry as is put into a press release, advertisement or sales brochure. New products and services can be highlighted, special offers can be made and readers can be urged to send for free booklets, research reports, tickets to free seminars, etc. The entry should be treated as another way of generating a response, and it is usually free. Exhibitors who only send in their name and address and a few desultory details are missing a free, or at worst, low-cost opportunity to sell after the show.

Seminars and conferences

Valuable publicity, and the ear of a very select audience, can often be gained by offering to organise a short seminar or conference on a subject of topical interest. Sometimes such an event will be initiated by the organiser and it is simply a question of supplying a speaker.

If such an opportunity is properly exploited there are advantages for all. The exhibitor gains exposure and will benefit from direct contact with the delegates attracted by the event. The organiser gains another reason for visitors to visit and a number of potential buyers who might otherwise not have come. The visitors can gain important information about new developments, whether technical, commercial or legal.

It is sad that at many such events the delegates' dissatisfaction is almost palpable due to the high level of overt selling by exhibitors over-anxious to capitalise on a captive audience with the result that seminars at exhibitions have a somewhat tarnished image. Exhibitors wishing to get the best from such events, whether arranged by them or as part of the organiser's programme should ensure that *all* the material presented is relevant, interesting, informative and as free from commercial hype as possible. For this reason a technical manager might well be a better choice for a speaker than a sales manager. The first objective should be to tell, not sell. In the skilful telling, a subtle selling (the best kind) takes place as the company is seen as helpful, informed and as impartial as is possible.

Press relations

Trade magazines will often print press releases received from advertisers. Some even sell advertisements and 'advertorial' (promotional material disguised as editorial matter) as a package.

Such publications can often be a poor choice for advertisers because if the real editorial or news is also compiled from press releases then the publication will have very little credibility with buyers, who will perceive it as biased, unreliable, and written for sellers, not buyers. This said, there are still some trade magazine editors who can be relied upon to be totally independent. Such editors select stories for their news rather than their commercial value and the readership of their publications, and the enhanced response they get to anything published, reflects this. It is worth while cultivating such contacts and finding out in more detail the kind of material they are looking for.

Press relations is something that many organisations can, and do, organise for themselves at low cost, although there are many PR companies that can assist with professional help, for a fee. Such companies tend to concentrate on writing press releases. But remember 99% of press releases end up as the contents of the editor's waste paper basket. See the two examples overleaf. Number 1 is how not to do it. Number 2 is a good example to copy.

It is often more effective for exhibitors to supply real newsworthy stories directly to the trade press. In exhibition terms this will probably mean stories about new products or services being launched at the show, or available for the first time buyers in the selected industry. Other viable news stories might be the initial user reaction to something being displayed at the show, the results of appropriate research or survey or a report on something happening at the stand such as a contest or visit by a well-known person or celebrity. Some exhibitors generate valuable coverage by having such 'happenings'.

Many at-show and post-show stories about large orders placed at the event are rigged and editors are fully aware of this. However if the order has genuinely been won from an overseas buyer in the teeth of ferocious competition from, for instance, American and Japanese competitors, then it stands a better chance. One UK exhibitor and wholesaler won an order from a Tokyo-based company, for leather goods made in China. The trade magazines carried the story – the value of the order, unknown to readers, was £83 and the samples, it eventually transpired, were required for copying!

Exhibitors wanting to get the best from the press should get a list of press contacts from the organiser, who will normally be happy to oblige on the basis that on average less than 10% of exhibitors bother with the press. After all, a mention of an exhibitor is also a mention for the show and some organisers will go even further, offering the services of their own press ofice to help identify possible stories and write the press releases. One unethical aspect of PR at exhibitions occurs when the press officer appointed by the organiser is an independent consultant but represents one or more of the exhibitors as well. In this situation journalists visiting the exhibition press office may find a biased selection of stories.

Press release number 1

Watford Widget Co.Ltd. *PRESS RELEASE*

WATFORD WIDGETS PULL IT OFF AGAIN!!

The Watford Widget Company Ltd, the worlds leading manufacturer of top quality, high precision widgets is pleased, nay proud to announce the long awaited launch of the new Wundawidget.

   The company will be exhibiting this miniaturised masterpiece of modern widgetry at Widgets 94.

   Chairman Bruce 'Bomber' Gusset, a war hero and pillar of his local Rotary club said: 'The new Wundawidget embodies the spirit of my firm, which I started in 1953 in a garden shed with £50 and an old bicycle for deliveries'.

   Sales and Marketing Director Jimmy 'Jimbo' Truss said: 'We believe in giving our customers tomorrow's technology today. This giant step forward for mankind will keep us on the cutting edge of business as we know it'.

Garden Works, North Villas, Watford, Herts.

This is an example of a very poor press release. It conveys nothing, and is puffy, verbose, irrelevant and sadly very common.

Press release number 2

Watford Widget Co.Ltd. *PRESS RELEASE*

<u>NEW WIDGET CUTS COST 30%</u>

Savings of up to 30% have been reported by early users of the new Wundawidget, just launched by the Watford Widget Co Ltd

Fred Blunt, chief buyer for British Mega said 'Since installing the Wundawidget in a number of our machines it seems that we are saving aound a third of our total production costs'.

Buyers can view a demonstration of the Wundawidget on stand 98 at Widgets 94 to be held at the Telford exhibition centre, March 9-11 1994

PRESS RELEASE

Garden Works, North Villas, Watford, Herts.

A good, crisp, sharp, press release which conveys a user benefit and an imperative, i.e. go to the exhibition and see a demonstration.

Press releases, announcements and invitations should be sent off in plenty of time for publication. For many monthly trade magazines, a full eight weeks lead time is not unusual and editors of overseas publications, possibly the most valuable of all, may need longer.

At the exhibition itself, press packs should be placed in the press office. Fifty is usually enough, but check with the organiser. These should contain a short release and, if relevant, a photograph packed into a clear plastic wallet so that both the picture, and the first paragraph of the release can be seen whilst the pack is still on the shelf. Journalists and editors are busy people and won't take things sealed up in brown envelopes marked 'Press'.

Keep checking the press office to make sure that your packs have not been shifted onto the floor, covered up by someone else's or removed by an unprincipled competitor as this has been known to happen. While there, take advantage of the opportunity to collect samples of the press packs of your competitors. Keep spare copies of your press packs on the stand for journalists who call.

Some exhibitors will hold a press conference at the event and this is something to consider if the news to be released is especially powerful, or if criticism needs to be answered. Check with the organiser to ensure that other events won't clash, and keep the conference short. For most journalists with only an hour or two to spare, a 30 minute session is more than enough and, despite reputations to the contrary, most journalists do not need expensive wining and dining to publish a story. Indeed amongst the press it is widely accepted that the quality of information presented at a press conference is generally in inverse proportion to the quality of hospitality offered.

Advertising

In terms of actually getting visitors to the stand, advertising can be the most expensive and least cost-effective method. Exhibitors often place ads in the special 'show-issue' of trade magazines, arguably the worst issue in which to advertise given the number of competitors doing the same. Such issues are often distributed at the event and are stuffed into visitors' carriers bags and brief cases, to be read on the way home. Many exhibitors simply modify their planned trade press advertising to a 'see you at the show – come to stand number forty-three' type of flash and this doesn't cost anything to do.

Better use can be made of trade journals, if they are actually exhibiting at the event and they often are, since the organiser will have traded a free stand for some general show advertising and editorial. One exhibitor at a motoring event ran a competition on the stand and persuaded three exhibiting trade magazines, with which he had placed substantial advertising, to distribute the competition forms free of charge. The forms had to be returned to the exhibitors stand, encouraging visits by people who might otherwise not have bothered.

Commonly, the organiser of an event will offer advertising in the exhibition catalogue and this needs to be considered carefully. If a substantial editorial entry is already included it may be superfluous. If advertising is taken it should be coded to enable identification of responses, and encourage responses from visitors reading the catalogue *after* the show. Responses can then be measured and an evaluation can be made. Too many exhibitors take advertising in the catalogue as a matter of course without really considering whether or not it works.

Advertising opportunities will also exist in the form of posters, banners, hot-air balloons and as part of computerised audio-visual presentations made to visitors at the show. These tend to be very difficult to evaluate. For most exhibitors, radio or television advertising will be inappropriate, as will advertising in the local or national press. One exception to this last point is the opportunity offered to exhibitors at Birmingham's NEC and in Brighton where the local papers prepare a special issue for distribution at the show with the front pages printed to carry commercial publicity written and presented to look like news stories.

Business gifts

Also known as 'give-aways' and in the USA as 'advertising specialties' these are items printed with a company name and given away by exhibitors at their events. Their effectiveness is often questionable when cheap, unwanted items are distributed indiscriminately on the basis of 'spreading the name'.

Relatively inexpensive items can however be effective if thoughtfully chosen. A pocket shoe-shine of the impregnated sponge variety, given

Evening Mail

TV PAGE 32
SPONSORED BY
Tyre Sales MOTORIST CENTRES

BRITAIN'S NEWSPAPER OF THE YEAR

THURSDAY, JUNE 11, 1992   25p

PRESENTED WITH THE COMPLIMENTS OF ...

E. K. Williams Limited

Victoria House, Victoria Street   Telephone 0942 816512
Westhoughton, Bolton   Facsimile 0942 814636
Lancashire BL5 3AR   Telex 635109 Chacom G EKW

VISIT US AT FORECOURT MARKETING & EQUIPMENT SHOW HALL 7/8 STAND H495

EKW TAKES TOP QUALITY AWARD

E K WILLIAMS Limited, the well-known firm of professional management accountants and business consultants, was presented with the coveted 'Esso Quest for Quality' award at the Forecourt Marketing and Equipment Show on Tuesday.

Mr Ray Gwilliams, Quality and Fuels Manager of ESSO, who presented the award, told the *Evening Mail*: "The reason we are here today is to recognise one particular contractor's achievements in the 'Quest for Quality'.

"E K Williams Limited was one contractor that not only managed to win the end of the year final award but also won each of its individual quarterly league finals.

"Therefore, it gives us great pleasure to present EKW with their award and we are absolutely delighted with the programme.

"It has proved the most effective way of improving our customer-satisfaction with the goods and services we provide to our retailers."

Hands-on

The 'ESSO Quest for Quality' award was accepted on behalf of EKW by Mr John Loeffen (General Manager, Europe), and Mr Mike Sinclair (UK Director).

EKW has been established since 1935 and, through its worldwide network of business consultants, prides itself on its ability to provide a highly informative, highly accurate and speedy service; enabling its clients to optimise their profitability.

"In the case of retailers, our systems and services provide a disciplined, hands-on approach to their profit maximisation," said Training and Marketing Manager, Mr Simon Lurie.

"In the case of oil companies or other organisations such as the British Franchise Association, our system works in support of their

financial requirements and programmes and provides the industry's statistics. In fact, we are the company that actually generates those statistics."

An important part of the EKW system is the provision of on-site monthly management accounts and, uniquely, a consultancy service to enable the retailer to have the discipline and control of any accounting system.

The service also covers the review and action stage too, to enable the client to maximise his profits under EKW guidance.

"In support of the monthly management accounts programme we also have a wide range of ancillary services. These include year end taxation, cash planning service

etc, which is the new service we are launching at the forecourt marketing & equipment show this year," said Sales Manager, Mr Neil Foster.

"Other services include payroll, polling, local account cards and electronic technological developments for the future."

Professional

In short, EKW provide a very professional and personal service to the retailer — including an expert to sit alongside him.

The excellent EKW system gives the client financial management control over his business in order for him to know what action to take and enables regular reviews

to be made. Unfortunately, many of the retailers who are visiting this show won't be in business tomorrow if they are not planning for their cash," said Mr Lurie.

"But our cash planning service has been tailored specifically to enable them to look ahead for the future.

"Without such, they will simply run out of cash in this recessionary period and, as businesses begin to expand, the activities of many of their competitors in hypermarkets will sink them."

Obviously, increased pressure from hypermarkets forms a serious threat to the unprepared retailer. EKW firmly expect that, in the not too distant future, hypermarket activities will scoop 20 per cent of the volume

across the whole of the UK.

"Let us not forget that in urban developments this could mean around 30 per cent volume disappearing," said Mr Lurie.

"As a result, many retailers will simply disappear and many of the forecourts will close.

Advice

"Moreover, we can now quite clearly see how that well-known prediction — of only 14,000 retail outlets being left by the end of the century — could indeed come forward!"

Obviously many visitors to the show fully agree with Mr Lurie's hard-hitting forecast. From the very first day of the show, the busy EKW

stand has attracted a considerable amount of interest from not only small retailers but also from major oil companies.

Of special interest is the friendly, E K Williams 'free advice shop', situated in Hall 6 (Stand A123).

"We were asked, by the organisers of the show, to participate in the free advice shop programme, and were delighted to do so," said Mr Foster.

"Therefore any retailer — or even oil company executives — can feel free to drop in and ask questions concerning any aspect of their own financial management.

"They can be sure that we will do our best to help them, with no obligations whatsoever."

AWARD: A plaque is presented to E K Williams Ltd, national finalist in Esso Quest for Quality '92. From left, Marketing Manager Simon Lurie, Director Mike Sinclair, Esso Quality Fuels Manager Ray Gwilliams, J W F Loeffen, General Manager (Europe), Esso Training Adviser Rupert Bravery and Sales/Services Manager Neil Foster

The Birmingham Evening Mail carrying commercial publicity written and presented as news.

away by hotels is useful and acceptable to most business types who travel. Single, beautifully wrapped, praline chocolates are used by a German exhibitor who finds that customers take them home for their partners. Small items for children are popular in some markets and small toys, cardboard models, badges, pocket mirrors, colourful posters, jigsaw puzzles and stickers have all been effectively used.

Some exhibitors prefer to give away a smaller number of more expensive items to selected visitors and good quality pens, diaries, pocketbooks, money clips, calculators and small leather goods are all welcomed, as are items used by the customer in the course of the job, such as slide rules for engineers or hand towels for doctors. One exhibitor, an airline, scored a hit with the 'Swiss Army Knife' a multi-blade, multi-tool, pocket knife with a distinctive trademark in the form of a white cross. Sadly the company lost a major customer from Saudi Arabia who took offence. The cross, a Christian symbol, is seen as an affront in Islamic countries and to an Arab, a gift of a knife or pair of scissors indicates 'I am cutting our relationship'. Gifts to be used overseas need to be approved by someone with knowledge of the local culture.

Points for Discussion

1 Suppose a small manufacturer of toys and games is about to exhibit at the annual trade show. How would you set about planning a pre-show direct mail campaign for this company?

2 Write the company's catalogue entry for the trade show.

3 Do you think the company should give away free gifts on the stand? If so, what should they be?

4 What sort of information would you include in the press pack? Which journalists would you try to meet?

5 Why do most press releases end up in an editor's bin?

6 What is wrong with press release number 1 on page 73? Why is press release number 2 on page 74 better?

CHAPTER EIGHT

WORKING THE STAND

This is the longest chapter in the book and, in many ways the most important. According to the Trade Show Bureau in the USA up to 80% of the success of an exhibition is in the hands of the stand staff. Exhibitions are a hands-on, people medium and it is often the best people at a show, not the best products or services, that run away with the prizes.

Working on an exhibition stand is not the same as selling. Sales skills are useful but the skills of generating leads by canvassing total strangers and dealing with a range of visitors are different, and therefore a different approach is needed. In fact, top sales performers can be a liability on a stand if they are unable to grasp the main differences.

1 *Dealing with suspects, not prospects*   Generally speaking most sales executives no longer make 'cold' calls, that is without appointments. Leads for appointments are generated by a number of methods including advertising, direct mail, PR and tele-marketing. The modern sales executive therefore, only deals with prospects who have been identified as potential buyers. At an exhibition the sales executive will have to talk to a large number of visitors of which only a small proportion will be prospects – the challenge is to find out which.

2 *Time*   A sales call can be relatively leisurely compared to an exhibition contact. Calls on customers and potential customers may last an hour or more. Five minutes is the usual goal to aim at with an exhibition contact, since the objective is normally to get them committed to an appointment at a later date and to collect

information rather than to sell. Many such possibilities will present themselves at a well-attended event and stand staff need to develop their conversational skills so that their organisation captures a worthwhile percentage of all the opportunities. A four day event attracting 10,000 visitors will deliver around 300 per hour, or five per minute past the stand. A member of staff spending 30 minutes on one visitor will be unable to talk to the other 150, some of whom may be better prospects.

The visitor's time, too, is precious. In the UK an average visit to an exhibition is one day since few visitors stay overnight due to the high prices of hotel rooms near most UK exhibition halls. Allowing for travelling time, the day is reduced to five hours and the majority of this time will be spent by the visitor on conversations with existing suppliers. Generally, less than two hours are allotted for discussions with potential suppliers. In a show comprising 600 exhibitors therefore, the likely time allotted per stand is just a few minutes.

The necessary 'compressing' of the exhibitor's presentation means that the normal sales approach will need to be modified, putting more emphasis on the benefits to be gained by using the products and services offered rather than on the personality of the sales person or the ethos of the company, unless these really are significant buyer benefits.

It should also be remembered that buying visitors are already in a state of heightened awareness about the products and services on display. Coming to the exhibition and being exposed to the sights and sounds has psychologically lifted them to a point where introductory small-talk or the social chit-chat usual in a longer sales call is likely to be downright annoying, as well as irrelevant. It's a business environment and exhibitor stand staff need to get down to business.

3 *Dealing with a range of visitors*   Sales executives generally visit clients but at an exhibition it is the stand staff who are visited; and stand staff have no control over who comes to the stand. Conversations will therefore take place with a variety of people, so approaches and techniques will need to be developed for dealing with them.

● **Students**   Students are the customers of the future and should be treated with courtesy. However, the commercial organisation is participating in the exhibition for short term goals – perhaps those achieveable within a year. To save time it therefore makes sense to develop student information sheets that can be handed out (see section on non-buying visitors in chapter 4) and for staff to be able to pass on the name of their organisation's personnel or public relations manager. Staff should be polite and warm, but brief.

● **The press**   The dangers of untrained staff talking to the press are considerable as some exhibitors have found out to their cost when they have been quoted. Ideally, professionally prepared press packs will be available in the exhibition press office but it is a good idea to keep a few on the stand to hand out. The press can be very supportive of the efforts of exhibitors but they do need special handling and it should be appreciated that they have their own objectives to fulfill. 'News' is often what someone, some-where would rather not see in print, so be careful!

● **Competitors**   An exhibition is an opportunity to uncover information about a competitor's products or services. This means that most exhibitors will be visited by their competitors and such visits will generally be counter-productive for the host, although many progressive sales managers maintain contact with their counterparts in other organisations and trade selected informa-tion, usually concerning clients. Generally competitors are easy to identify by their depth of knowledge of the industry, or of the host's business. The types of questions asked with regard to technical improvements on discounts will often identify them. 'Consultants' are commonly used to probe for commercial information.

● **Suppliers**   Some sales executives visit shows to sell to the exhibitors. Stand staff should be briefed to simply collect literature for passing on and to get rid of the visitors as soon as possible. The investment in the stand has been made for selling, not buying.

● **Staff and ex-staff**   Some of the most time-wasting conversa-tions take place with staff from other parts of the exhibitor's organisation. One large company forbids such staff to visit its stand to update their knowledge of the product but puts on a special annual event for this purpose. Ex-staff wishing to catch up on company gossip should be relegated to a meeting time after the show.

● **Complainers**   For the complainant there is no more public arena in which to air a complaint, and possibly cause maximum embarrassment and damage, than an exhibition stand. Faced with such a situation a member of staff should suggest discussing the subject away from the stand, preferably in a catering area where the complainant can be sat down and given some simple hospitality such as tea or coffee. The member of staff should make it clear that he or she is *not* the person who can solve the problem but simply wants to help by getting the complainant's name and telephone number so that they can be quickly contacted by the appropriate person in the organisation. One skilled exhibitor gained a lot of credibility from such a situation by telephoning his technical director in front of the complainant and passing on the details. Complainants handled well can turn into loyal clients.

● **Non-buying juniors**   A sales director of a multi-national complex company once commented to the press: 'I'm not here to be polite to people who can't buy. I've got a business to run'. He was wrong of course. Courtesy costs nothing and it can pay off, particularly with non-buying staff who may have an indirect influence on the purchase or the ear of the buyer. One exhibitor, a few years ago, spent five or ten minutes giving information about his products to a twenty year old trainee account executive from a small provincial advertising agency. The brochures were taken back to the agency account director who saw a potential use for one of his clients and subsequently called the supplier in to tender. The resulting order, valued at £86,000 paid the exhibitor's expenses a hundred times over.

Treating juniors with the disdain suggested by the sales director's comment is a good way for exhibitors to deprive themselves of potential sales, both immediate and future. Juniors, in the course of time, become seniors.

Secretaries and personal assistants can also be helpful and often have far greater influence on their bosses than the latter would admit. Exhibitors should seek out every opportunity to make a good impression on such contacts and expand their network of friends.

● **Customers**   Strange though it may appear at first, customers can sometimes be a libility to the exhibitor, especially if the real objective is to make new business contacts. Some exhibitors detail selected staff to spend time with customers. One solution to the time problem might be to arrange a special event for customers (see section on hospitality in chapter 5).

Generally the ideal approach is that the time at the exhibition is limited and that it is best spent uncovering new sources of business. Spending large amounts of time chatting to competitors, students, suppliers, the press, staff, ex-staff, or even customers is unlikely to be as productive as spending time with potential customers.

It is also worth remembering that visitors to an exhibition tend to come in three distinct categories according to a well-known training film called 'How Not To Exhibit Yourself' by Video Arts. These are: the very interested, the totally disinterested and the possibly interested, or the 'fringe voters'.

The very interested will, for whatever reason, walk on to the stand of their own free will and may require further information, or a demonstration. The disinterested simply will not come.

It is the 'possibles' passing by that represent the greatest potential, and challenge. Stand staff will need to develop skilled canvassing techniques in order to stop, evaluate and subsequently spend a few minutes with those that can buy, with the objective of getting a sale (if relevant) or more likely an appointment, or a commitment to make an appointment at a later date. The skills of canvassing are generally learnt on the stand, in a live situation, but here are some basic steps that should first be considered by all stand staff.

Initial contact

The best way for stand staff to attract the attention of passing visitors is to look them in the eye, smile and say something. The eye contact is a very important element in getting, and holding, the complete attention of the visitor just for that important second or two. From the visitor's point of view it is almost impossible, and certainly churlish, to avoid someone who is looking them in the eye and saying something, especially if delivered with a friendly smile.

The initial contact stage lasts two or three seconds and this will be long enough to include a simple polite greeting such as 'good morning' or 'good afternoon'. The addition of 'sir' or 'madam' is a matter of personal preference.

The objective is to simply catch the attention of the visitor, and stop him or her walking past the stand. This gives the exhibitor a chance to deliver the all important opening line.

Stand staff will need to select those visitors that they feel are worth stopping and a word of warning is appropriate here. Most in the UK will choose men in their 40s dressed in suits, believing that such are more likely to be serious buyers. This is a serious error. Increasingly, women are becoming buyers and decision-influencers, and most stand staff ignore them. Young people can hold senior positions and people of any age may have deliberately dressed casually in order to be left alone. Stand staff also lose potentially valuable export opportunities when they avoid, as they commonly do, anyone foreign-looking.

The author's prize for one of the worst approaches in history was awarded at an Incentives exhibition where a young salesman, watched by his grinning colleagues, sauntered towards two women, who were standing admiring the display and opened up with: 'Well, what can we show you girls, then?' One of the two 'girls' (who turned out to be senior buyers for a major consumer goods company) cut him dead with an icy look and they both quickly left.

It would be fair to say that, on average, stand staff do a poor job when it comes to approaching visitors. The National Exhibitors Association (NEA) conducted a survey of a financial exhibition where stand staff were expected to be professional, motivated and skilled at handling people. The association sent a 40-year-old white male in a suit to walk slowly past the stands and note how he was approached, if at all. The results, given below will be sufficient to convince those spending money on exhibitions how vital good stand staff really are, and how destructive bad ones can be.

The time selected was 2.30 pm on the second day of the three-day event, and the responses from each stand were as follows:

- A reasonable start, visitor asked: 'Would you like some details of our new product?'

- Visitor ignored at first, then 'Good morning.' (remember, it was 2.30 pm).

- Three salesmen drinking beer, visitor looked at but ignored.

- Man smoking a pipe: 'Can we help you, then?'

- Woman watching her own company video on stand, and ignoring all visitors.

- Four stand staff sitting drinking: 'Can we help you?'

- Good. Friendly smile and eye contact: 'What can we show you?'

- Very large, expensive stand, completely empty.

- Visitor ignored.

- Visitor ignored, staff all smoking and drinking at back of stand.

- Very large expensive stand, with a glamorous hostess filing her fingernails and ignoring visitors.

- Good. Stand staff stopped visitor gently and asked: 'Are you attending the conference?'

- Visitor ignored by staff sitting drinking.

- Fair, visitor stopped and asked: 'Have you seen something you like?'

- Visitor ignored, at a very large, expensive and visually stunning stand. Staff sitting reading newspapers and drinking coffee.

- Visitor ignored by staff sitting and watching visitors pass.

- Visitor giving eye contact and a smile, then ignored.

- Good. Visitor stopped and asked. 'Are you a conference delegate?'

- Visitor given eye contact, and a smile. 'Can I help you?'

- Salesman sitting down made eye contact with the visitor, then rose slowly and said: 'Can I help you?'

- Excellent. Visitor gently stopped and asked the nature of their business and their interest in the exhibition.

- Visitor stopped with an interesting opening line: 'What effect do you think the election will have on our industry?'

- Visitor ignored by two salesmen sitting reading newspapers on a large, expensive stand.

- Visitor given eye contact by salesman who then broke it and turned away. The salesman then turned back to face the aisle when the visitor had gone.

- Visitor ignored by three salesmen who were talking to each other.

- Visitor given eye contact and a smile, but nothing said.

- Good. Visitor stopped gently and asked: 'Are you a buyer of this type of service?'

- Visitor given eye contact and 'Can I help you?'

- Visitor ignored by six salesmen on a large stand who ignored most visitors.

- Excellent. Visitor stopped and asked: 'Would you like to know how you can save money with our new service?'

- Visitor given eye contact by all three salesmen on the edge of the stand. One smiled and said: 'Good afternoon' but nothing else.

- Good, visitor told: 'You're looking interested.'

- Good, visitor given eye contact and smile and asked: 'Would you like to win a free bottle of champagne?'

- Visitor ignored by a salesman sitting reading a newspaper.

- Stand empty.

- Good. Visitor stopped and asked: 'Are you a buyer of these services?'

- Stand empty.

- Visitor ignored by stand staff talking to each other.

- Fair. Visitor stopped and asked: 'Are you coming to see us?'

- Visitor asked: 'Can we help you at all?'

- Good. Visitor asked: 'Are you involved in this market?'

- Excellent. Visitor stopped and asked: 'Have you had your free copy of this?'

Given the above it seemed that only one in four of the exhibitors was making any attempt to open a conversation. Many were guilty of habits and attitudes that were positively repelling visitors.

Opening lines

The challenge for most stand staff is to find some effective ways of opening conversations without using the common and virtually useless 'Can I help you?' a question which attracts the answer 'No thanks I'm just looking.' In general terms open ended questions – those that cannot be answered with a simple 'yes' or 'no' are the safest best.

Staff should avoid questions which begin conversations on a social note. 'Small talk' is fine for sales conversations in buyers' offices but to the majority of visitors who are in a hurry, it is merely irritating. Since the visitor knows the exhibitor is there for business it can also sound annoyingly false.

The best opening lines are those which encourage the visitor to talk about business (the reason for all the parties being there) and a simple: 'What brings you to the exhibition today?' or 'What do you think of the show?' may be sufficient to get visitors to reveal their reasons for attending. Staff for one international hotel chain open conversations with: 'When was the last time you stayed in a really good hotel?' Note the use of the word *you* in all these examples, and in the good opening lines listed above.

Another technique, using a carefully structured, closed-ended question, is to simply ask the visitor if they buy, and allow them to move on with just a nod and a smile if they don't. Something along the lines of: 'Does your organisation currently use ...' and/or 'Are you involved in buying or specifying . . .' can lead straight into a presentation if the answer is 'yes'. Closed-ended questions, skilfully worded and well presented can quickly separate potential customers from passing visitors.

Some other examples of possible opening lines are given below. Stand staff can adapt those with an X to their own requirements.

- 'Are you enjoying the conference?'

- 'We've found a new way to solve the X problem. Is this something you need to do?' (note the word *new*)

- 'Our new X can cut production time by as much as 30%. Are you involved in buying X?'

- 'Do you use X?'

- 'What kind of X do you currently use?'

- 'Would a saving of 30% on X be of interest to you?'

- 'Have you had one of our free research reports on the problems of X?'

- 'Are you familiar with the savings/improvements you can make by using X?'

- 'Do the X's you are currently stocking give you a 50% margin?'

- 'Does your present system allow you to X?'

- 'When did you install your current X?'

- 'What return are you enjoying from your current X?'

- 'Our X is currently used by (name large company using product). Are you familiar with its advantages?'

- 'We're demonstrating the new X on the stand today. Are you involved in buying or specifying these?'

- 'How much are you currently paying for X?'

- 'If I could show you how to X would you be interested?'

- 'How does your organisation currently X?'

- 'Are you looking for something that will X?'

- 'What features of an X are important to you?'

- 'What models of X do you stock at the moment?'

- 'Where do you currently buy X?'

- 'Which method of solving the X problem do you currently use?'

- How is the new EC directive on X affecting you?

No member of the stand staff should attempt to stop visitors without having thought through some basic 'openers' as above, and the likely course of the conversations thereafter.

The other need for opening lines will be apparent when visitors come on to the stand voluntarily and are looking at some aspect of it. Staff will often either hover annoyingly, like badly trained retail shop assistants or approach immediately with a 'Can I help you?' Neither are helpful. Customers should be given around 15 seconds to get their bearings, (time it – it's long enough) and then be approached directly with a sensible 'icebreaker' chosen from the list above. Another opening gambit could be something along the lines of 'I'm just over here if you have any questions.'

If appropriate, reference can easily be made to the item being studied as in:

- 'I see our X caught your eye'

- 'Are you involved in buying X then?'

- 'Was it the texture of our X that attracted you?'

- 'Would you like more information on X?'

- 'It's only £59 a hundred and we can deliver in seven days.'

- 'Have you seen that particular feature before?'

- 'What especially interested you in our X?'

- 'Have you seen our demonstration/video?'

Identification

Having made contact and opened the conversation, and assuming that it is with a potential customer, it will now be necessary for the member of stand staff to find out the name of the potential customer.

This is most easily accomplished by handing him or her a business card with a request to 'exchange details', or a simple 'May I take your business card/name and address?' Buyers are sometimes reticent about exposing themselves in this way and this may be due to a fear of being pestered at a later date. If a request for a business card is met with a blunt refusal however, it could mean that the visitor is not a genuine buyer but a competitor, especially if they stopped on the stand voluntarily. On this basis it is best for stand staff to proceed warily and not to spend too much time with the visitor. A few sentences of explanation about the product or service and another request for identification is the most appropriate action. This second request could be justified by an explanation such as there being extra information, not available on the stand ('It's confidential – we don't want our competitors getting it') and that this can be sent on after the show, hence the need for a name and address. If this fails it might be best to give the visitor whatever brochures are available and appropriate and politely terminate the conversation. Generally speaking only a tiny minority will refuse to give their details. In fact some professional buyers carry briefing sheets detailing what they buy and when and hand these out to potential suppliers at exhibitions.

Presentation

There are many skills involved in selling and much has been written about the psychology of the process. The novice will blunder in with a list of product features. The experienced seller will ask carefully framed questions designed to reveal what the customer is looking for, aspects that (surprise!) just happen to be noted features of whatever is being sold.

The sale of a car is a good example. Customers enter the car showroom and the experienced sales executive will sit them down and *will not* show them any cars until some probing has been done. Is speed important? Fuel consumption? Comfort? Size? Running costs? Total cost? Reliability? Safety? Are extras like stereos, air conditioning, sunroofs, metallic paint, racing wheels, tow-bars or luggage racks important? How many people will be using it? What sort of mileage will it be doing? What is the customer driving now? Is this a trade-up, or a trade-down? Is there a trade-in? Will the company pay? And so on.

The questions are pertinent and even flattering. The experienced sales executive also uses the customer's name a few times in the conversation. And the word *you* is used a lot ('Is price per mile important to you Mr Jones?') The answers are mentally ticked off against the cars actually available until the final announcement ('I think this is what you're looking for Mr Jones').

The point of the questions is that they keep control in the hands of the seller. There may be dozens or even hundreds of aspects to a company and the product or service being sold and whilst some aspects or benefits will be important in the buyer's mind, others will be less important. By asking questions the few important ones can be revealed, and the company, product or service can then be presented in terms of this specification.

It is worth spending some time reviewing the potential benefits of your company's product just before an exhibition as this builds confidence. The following list is intended as a guide to this process – not all the aspects will apply but a few could be selected for each type of customer. For instance if the product was a fork-lift truck then a factory manager might be especially interested in its safety, the operator in comfort and buyer in its price.

Benefits list

Labour-saving
Time-saving
Money-saving
Safety features
Cost aspect (capital or running)
Durability
Quality
Guarantees and warranties
Money back offers
Award winning
Recommended by
Used by

Choice of colours, models and styles
Payment terms
Delivery times
Service contract
High security
Speed of operation/ cycle
Ease of use – user friendliness
Training given
After sales service
Technical back-up
Research programme

Where made
Number of local depots/outlets
Size of company – large enough to cope
Size of company – small enough to care
Produced by British Standards (Do you have BS 5750?)
Environmentally friendly

Status bestowed	High profit margin on	Size of item
Adaptability	re-sale	(miniaturisation)
Range of accessories	Limited edition	Quantity discounts
Specialist company	Association with	Physical qualities:
(not a 'jack of all	famous persons	flame-retardent,
trades')	('by appointment')	weatherproof,
Exclusivity (only	Exported	rust-proof, non-
selected customers)	Financial strength of	slip, non-fade,
	firm	washable

Many additions to this list can of course be made, but it can serve as a prompt for all stand staff needing to review exactly what the major benefits of using the product or service are.

There are a number of other aspects to be considered when talking to potential buyers on an exhibition stand and which are particularly relevant to this type of selling, but may also have a wider application. These are outlined in the following list.

- Don't launch into the jargon of the industry until the level of the buyer's knowledge has been ascertained. Remember that many visitors to exhibitions are non-technical but may still have a significant effect on the placing of orders.

- Don't talk down to juniors. We were all junior once and juniors have memories.

- Try to be seen as a teller, not a seller. Avoid the obvious and well-known selling ploys, such as answering a question with a question: 'Will it knock 20% off my product costs?' 'If I can prove that it does are you going to buy it?'

- Avoid clichés. 'As you know Mr Buyer, these days you have to speculate to accumulate.'

- Don't talk while the buyer is reading copy or watching a demonstration or a video.

- The proportion of buyer/seller conversation should be 75% buyer, 25% seller.

- Don't criticise competing companies whether they're at the show or not.

- Use words such as *new*, *free*, *you*, *your*.

- The question *when* can be a powerful way of finding out if the visitor is really serious about making a purchase or just collecting information: e.g. 'When would you need to install the system', 'When would you need to buy to get the purchase into this year's budget?'

- Beware of negative body language. Standing with arms folded, hands crossed, in front of your body, or sprawled in a chair is unlikely to engender confidence.

- Wear badges high on the right, so that they can be seen when you shake hands.

- If selling a product, persuade the visitor to take a hands-on approach and touch it as soon as possible. Touching creates familiarity and confidence.

- Don't group with other stand staff, or talk to them when visitors are passing. Opportunities at exhibitions are fleeting and can easily be missed.

- Make notes of what visitors say – it's flattering to the buyers and essential information for the sellers. Let the visitor see the enquiry form.

- Don't break eye contact to look over the visitor's shoulder at other visitors. Sellers should interrupt their own conversations, not those of their visitors, if they have to say 'I'll be with you in a moment'.

- Don't eat, drink or smoke on the stand, or sit down, unless it's with a visitor.

- Wear comfortable shoes. Remember that exhibition stand work means standing for long periods. Feet can swell a whole shoe size so choose soft leather lace-ups. If you are going to be standing on concrete floors 'cushion-sole' shoes save a lot of pain.

- Late nights out don't help.

- Curries and garlic bread taste great but linger on the breath and are released through the skin in perspiration. Save such foods for after the exhibition.

- A 'freshen-up' kit can be a good friend at a show. Perfume, aftershave, mouthwash, toothbrush and paste, and deodorant can all act as a 'pick-me-up.' Some experienced professionals also use eye-baths.

- Glucose tablets are good for quick energy.

- Alcohol costs sales.

- A clipboard can be a good friend at an exhibition. It's something to keep your hands occupied, can hold enquiry pads, pens, leaflets and business cards and is a writing surface.

- Take regular breaks and sit down away from the stand. Stay fresh.

Finishing the conversation

The conversation will usually conclude with one of four things being agreed: an order taken, an appointment made, an agreement to call for an appointment, a promise to send further information. From the seller's point of view it is desirable to obtain an appointment whilst the buyer is actually on the stand since many promises made by buyers to sellers are later broken. If stand staff are also the sales team they should be equipped with their business diaries so that appointments can be made. If stand staff are not the executives who will eventually make the call, the appointment should still be made at a time convenient to the buyer and then someone from sales found to keep the appointment.

The follow-up is an essential aspect of any exhibition. The leads generated will have been won at some considerable cost; in picking the right show, choosing the best site and designing, promoting and managing the stand as professionally as possible. If leads are not followed up, and regrettably many are not, all this effort has been wasted.

The stand staff and their actions at the show are a very important component of the lead-generation process. Those responsible for converting the leads into sales are ultimately responsible for generating the money that will pay for it all.

Points for Discussion

1 With a partner, role-play a situation in which you are a paper manufacturer running the stand at a trade show and your partner is an interested potential buyer. How might the conversation proceed? After the first run-through, reverse your roles.

2 How long are most exhibition contacts – what is the usual goal?

3 Think up five good opening lines for the above show.

4 How would you deal with a competitor who showed up on your stand pretending to be a visiting buyer?

5 How do you think a company might organise their follow-up procedures after a major exhibition?

6 What would be the ten worst mistakes stand staff could make?

EXHIBITING OVERSEAS

For many UK organisations exhibitions represent one of the best ways of promoting goods and services in overseas markets.

There are a number of reasons for this. In the first instance an exhibition might be the only viable way to reach the market other than with a sales force. Direct mail or advertising may be unavailable or not sufficiently well developed in the selected country to be worth considering.

The culture of the country and the way its buyers do business might also be a factor. In some areas such as the Middle and Far East great emphasis is placed on personal contact and the more impersonal, detached forms of marketing may be inappropriate. Some countries, such as Germany, have a long tradition of doing business at exhibitions and many of its fairs are amongst the largest and most successful trade events in the world.

A third aspect of UK overseas exhibiting, is the help and financial support available from the DTI and various other trade associations to exhibitors at overseas shows. Most marketing managers looking at a first tentative step into an overseas market would be well advised to consider exhibiting as part of a British 'section'. The benefits can be considerable and not just in purely financial savings, but also in being steered through all the official form-filling, in avoiding potential disasters, in being part of a large stand with its facilities and its impact on visitors and media and in having someone else manage the project. Later, as the organisation gains a foothold, and experience, consideration can be given to 'going it alone'.

In terms of marketing strategy, an overseas event can represent the most effective way for an organisation to break into a new market. The audience is select, interested and delivered in large numbers during a short time-span. Demonstrations can be made, prototypes can be shown and market research carried out. A complex product or service which is difficult to depict, can also be easily exposed. Overseas agents can be found – indeed many organisations exhibit just to find and employ such valuable staff, who then direct future exhibition strategy.

Other benefits are also enjoyed by overseas exhibitors, including the fact that it can sometimes be cheaper than exhibiting in the UK, even when flights and freight are taken into account. Secondly, the presence of an organisation in an overseas exhibition will invariably be noticed by those UK buyers attending as visitors. Valuable contacts can be made with the UK's largest companies as buyers will often stop to talk to UK exhibitors, if only out of politeness or to hear a voice from home.

However, despite all this optimism, one is frequently advised by experienced overseas exhibitors not to expect too much from the first event. It may take several exhibitions, perhaps spread over a number of years, to establish the organisation in an overseas market, especially those where the cultures are so different to that of the UK such as the Middle East, Far East, and South America, not to mention Eastern Europe, France and Italy nearer to home.

The increasing influence of the European Community, will have a significant effect on the exhibition activities of many UK organisations looking to export, perhaps for the first time. Few will be able to ignore exhibitions overseas and many will need to find additional budgets for this area of expenditure, or modify their UK programmes.

Overseas exhibitions – the differences

Adjusting to necessary changes is paramount when doing business overseas as exhibitions reflect the customs and culture of the host country. On the purely practical side exhibition space is expressed in square feet in the USA and Australia and in square metres in Europe. Electrical connections and regulations will be different as will regulations affecting the height and the construction of the stand. Exhibition timings may vary. In the Middle East

British section at an overseas exhibition

a show will close for the afternoon and re-open for the evening, which is commonly the busiest time. In some Eastern European countries very long events lasting ten days or more, are normal. In this instance, some British exhibitors, having had seven days of giving away literature and free samples to seemingly endless numbers of young visitors, fly home early, not appreciating that the juniors were advance scouts for more senior buyers, who, having studied all the literature brought back, visit the show to place orders during its last days.

The attitude of the commercial world to its exhibitions in various countries is worth noting. In the UK it is unusual for more than 10% of an organisation's total marketing budget, (which includes advertising, direct mail, PR etc) to be spent on exhibitions. In Germany a figure of 20–30% is fairly common.

The sheer scale of German exhibitions is an indication of the importance placed on them by both business and government and is perhaps also a consequence of the geographical centrality of Germany and the excellent network of road, rail and air communications. Over 100 major international events take place there every year, in which 100,000 exhibitors participate (40,000 from overseas). More than 8 million visitors attend, of which 1.3 million come from outside Germany, about half coming from other EC countries. All the exhibition halls in the UK could be fitted into the Hannover complex, just one of Germanys exhibition centres, with room to spare.

In other countries, such as the USA, the size of the companies and the scale of their budget means that some companies have full-time exhibition specialists dedicated to the exhibition programme. In the USA where the exhibition budget per company is several times greater than in the UK, there are an estimated 3,000 exhibit managers. In the UK, where companies are smaller and the commitment is less there are a few hundred. The role is usually undertaken by someone from marketing, sales or PR, on a part-time basis.

The stand strategy and design will also need to be carefully considered. In Germany buyers often expect to place orders at shows. Exhibitors will often therefore, build large stands and entertain on them. Buyers may stay for hours. In the USA, perhaps because of the tax that the US government demands from shows where exhibitors sell, the emphasis is on lead-generation and buyers are quickly identified, processed and gently sent on their way, all in a few minutes. The order is then obtained from the follow-up call. The stand design will reflect these differences and also take into account cultural expectations with regard to shapes, colours, graphics and accessories.

In these respects it is easy to get it wrong. The wrong colours or flowers used can suggest death or other inappropriate messages to visitors, and 'glamour' pictures of women, or alcoholic drinks on stands are sure to offend in the Arab world. It is also worth remembering that some nationalities read text from right to left and that sequences of photographs may need to be reversed. Lines on graphs, especially if designed to show an upward trend can easily be misunderstood. Bright primary colours are popular in Germany, pastels are preferred in France.

Slogans will need to be chosen with care as they may be subject to misinterpretation. At one German merchandise fair some UK exhibitors were using special stickers for some products which said 'Ideal business gift'. The word gift in German means poison. At the same show a German manufacturer offering saucepans in bright primary colours was startling the British and American buyers by proclaiming that the cookware was 'especially designed for gay people'. It is worth having all copy translated back into the original language to ensure that barriers to selling are not being set up.

In general the best advice is to put the effort and money into the product and services to be displayed and the people working on the stand, rather than putting it into an expensive stand design. Doubling the expenditure on the stand design may not result in a single extra contact, but the employment of good local canvassers who speak the language can make all the difference.

The following advice is also relevant to overseas events.

- Book accommodation as early as possible.

- Have the sales staff fly out ahead of time, to get over jet lag, familiarise themselves and set up appointments. Plan for them to stay after the show has finished to follow up leads.

- In some countries even 'harmless' general interest magazines can be seen as offensive.

- In Arab countries the role of women in business is a far smaller one than in most other parts of the world.

● In hot countries audio-visual equipment often malfunctions.

● Shipping can represent a considerable cost. Check if displays can be sold, left with agents or even destroyed if the cost of getting them home is prohibitive. Some exhibitors pre-sell equipment displayed at exhibitions, to avoid shipping costs and to help pay the cost of exhibiting.

● Use designers and contractors with specific experience of the country chosen wherever possible.

● Note telephone numbers of people who could be vital *before* leaving the UK. A list might include: the freight agent's local representative, the Commercial Attaché at the British Embassy or Consulate, the travel agent's local representative, the local agent's senior personnel (home numbers), the co-ordinating officer's hotel number (if on a DTI group stand), alternative contractors.

● Take lots of extra brochures. Some exhibitors recommend two or three times the number taken for UK events.

● Gifts, especially if unique to the UK can be very useful as give-aways. In some countries such items as ordinary as ballpoint pens, cigarettes and even pairs of jeans can be very valuable.

● Arrange to be able to draw cash from a local bank or one in the exhibition hall.

● Remember that copyright and patent laws vary from country to country. In some areas in the Far East the worst strategy is to expose a successful product to copying.

● Translated copy can take up more or less space than English. English is about the same as Italian and French but Russian, German and Spanish could need 15–20% more space.

Points for Discussion

1 Why are overseas exhibitions one of the best ways of promoting your organization overseas?

2 Which government department is responsible for providing financial help and practical support for companies exhibiting?

3 What is *the* major difference between buying practice at overseas exhibitions in Germany and USA?

4 What are the alternatives to paying heavy shipping costs to bring equipment display material home?

5 Do you think that the government should increase subsidies to UK companies exhibiting in the EC?

CONCLUSION

Exhibitions offer enormous opportunities to those who know how to get the best from them, in terms of show and site selection, stand design, publicity and staffing. However, for others, exhibitions will remain an enigma; a confusing mix of marketing strategy, PR, advertising tactics and street-trader selling techniques.

I am often asked: 'What makes a good exhibitor?' Exhibitions are best exploited by those who are good at dealing with people – if you don't get on with people you'll hate exhibitions.

Good exhibitors also tend to be practical people who enjoy 'hands-on' marketing and coming face to face with customers.

When travelling in a strange land a good map is essential. I hope that this book provides adequate guidance for new exhibitors by charting the pitfalls, and more positively, highlighting the kind of good practice that will produce successful exhibitors in the 1990s.

UK TRADE
PUBLICATIONS

Conference and Exhibition
Fact Finder/Data Book
Batiste Publications
Pembroke House
Campsbourne Road
Hornsey
London N8 7PE
☎ 081 340 3291

Exhibiting/Exhibition File/
Exhibition Organiser
Exhibitor Services
29a Market Square
Biggleswade
Bedforshire
SG18 8AQ
☎ 0767 316255

Exhibitions and Conferences
70 Abingdon Road
London
W8 6AP
☎ 071 937 6636

Exhibition Bulletin
266–272 Kirkdale
Sydenham
London
SE26 4RZ
☎ 081 778 2288

Exhibition Management
FMJ International Publications Ltd
Queensway House
2 Queensway
Redhill
Surrey
RH1 1QS
☎ 0737 768611

The Marketplace
PO Box 229
Sutton
Surrey
SU1 3TP
☎ 081 643 8415

TRAINING FILMS

UK TRADE ASSOCIATIONS

National Exhibitors Association
29a Market Square
Biggleswade
Bedfordshire
SG18 8AQ
☎ 0767 316255

Video Arts
68 Oxford Street
London
W1N 9LA
☎ 071 637 7288

Association of Exhibition Organisers
417 Market Towers
Nine Elms Lane
London
SW8 5NQ
☎ 071 627 3946

British Exhibition Contractors Association
Kingsmere House
Graham Road
Wimbledon
London
SW19 3SR
☎ 081 543 3888

British Exhibition Venues Association
Mallards
Five Ashes
Mayfields
East Sussex
TN20 6NN
☎ 0435 872244

Exhibition Industry Federation
Sheen Lane House
Upper Richmond Road
London
SW14 8AG
☎ 081 878 9130

USA TRADE PUBLICATIONS

National Association of Exhibition Hallowners
G-Mex Centre
Manchester
M2 3GX
☎ 061 834 2700

National Exhibitors Association
29a Market Square
Biggleswade
Bedfordshire
SG18 8AQ
☎ 0767 316255

Incorporated Society of British Advertisers
44 Hertford Street
London
W1Y 8AE
☎ 071 499 7502

Exhibitor
745 Marquette Bank Building
Rochester, MN 55903
☎ 507/289-6556

Exhibit Builder
P.O. Box 4144
Woodlands Hills, CA 91365
☎ 800/356-4451

Successful Meetings
633 Third Avenue
New York, NY 10017
☎ 212/986-4800

Tradeshow and Convention Guide
49 Music Square West
Nashville, TN 37203
☎ 615/321-4250

Tradeshow & Exhibit Manager
Goldstein & Associates
1150 Yale Street
Suite 12
Santa Monica, CA 90403
☎ 213/828-1309

Tradeshow Week Publications
12233 W. Olympic Boulevard
Suite 236
Los Angeles, CA 90064
☎ 213/826-5696

USA TRADE ASSOCIATIONS

Exhibit Designers and Producers Association
611 E. Wells Street
Milwaukee, WI 53202
☎ 414/276-3372

Exposition Service Contractors Association
400 S. Houston Street
Union Square
Dallas, TX 75202
☎ 214/744-9902

International Exhibitors Association
5103-B Backlick Road
Annandale, VA 22003
☎ 703/941–3725

National Association of Exposition Managers
334 E. Garfield Road
P.O. Box 377
Aurora, OH 44202
☎ 216/562–8255

Trade Show Bureau
P.O. Box 797
8 Beach Road
East Orleans, MA 02643
☎ 508/240-0177

EXHIBITION DISPLAY SUPPLIERS

Academy Exhibitions Ltd
Academy House
Unit 6, Capital Place
Stafford Road
Croydon, CR0 4TU
☎ 081 667 0307

Advertising Constructions
2/4 Howard Place
Shelton
Stoke on Trent
Staffs, ST1 4NQ
☎ 0782 264465

Cornerways Exhibitions
23 Rookwood Way
Haverhill
Suffolk, CB8 9PA
☎ 0440 703048

Clip Ltd
Avon Works
Wick
Bristol
Avon, BS15 5PE
☎ 0275 822636

Dimensions 8 Limited
Dimension House
20 Leeway
Newport
Gwent, NP9 0SL
☎ 0633 270808

Displaylines Ltd
15 River Park
Ampere Road
Newbury
Berkshire, RG13 2DQ
☎ 0635 528103

**Display Systems
International Ltd**
3 Victoria Wharf
Victoria Road
Dartford
Kent, DA1 5AJ
☎ 0322 222474

Expo Portable Display Ltd
10 Georgiana Street
London, NW1 0EF
☎ 071 282 4004

Expotechnik
Hudnall Lane
Little Gaddesden
Berkhamsted
Herts
HP4 1QE
☎ 044284 2515

Foga/Norking Aluminium Ltd
LKH Estate
Tickhill Road
Balby
Doncaster
S. Yorks
DN4 8QG
☎ 0302 855907

Leitner GB
254 Wellingborough Road
Northampton
NN1 4EJ
☎ 0604 230445

Marler Haley Exposystems Ltd
Beaconsfield Close
Hatfield
Herts
AL10 8XB
☎ 07072 68155

Matrix Display Equipment
Olympia House
26 Clothier Road
Brislington
Bristol
BS4 5PT
☎ 0272 772278

Modular Displays Ltd
19a Water Lane
Wilmslow
Cheshire
SK9 5AE
☎ 0625 533555

Nexo Display Systems Ltd
5 Over Minnis
New Ash Green
Dartford
Kent
DA3 8JA
☎ 0474 873512

Nimlok Ltd
Head Office:
Unit 9
Baron Avenue
Telford Way Industrial Estate
Kettering
Northants
NN16 8UW
☎ 0536 515459

Panelflex
Barton Hall
Hardy Street
Eccles
Manchester
M30 7WA
☎ 061 707 6076

Pillory Barn Exhibitions
Unit 20
Potts Marsh
Eastbourne Road
Westham
Pevensey
E. Sussex
BN24 5NH
☎ 0323 460600

Promotional World (Modular Systems) Ltd
254 Wellingborough Road
Northampton
NN1 4EJ
☎ 0604 230445

RT Display Systems Ltd
212 New Kings Road
SW6 4NZ
☎ 071 731 4181

Roadstar Expo Ltd
18a Duppas Hill Road
Croydon
Surrey
CR0 4BG
☎ 081 688 8467

S.D. Systems Ltd
Unit 2
Cressex Business Complex
Lancaster Road
High Wycombe
HP12 3NN
☎ 0494 465212

Snap Display Systems
7 Golf Road
Bromley
Kent
BR1 2JA
☎ 081 468 7140/1

Speedscreen Modular Display Systems
PO Box 15
176 Back High Street
Gosforth
Newcastle upon Tyne
Tyne and Wear
NE3 1JF
☎ 091 284 6536

Standeasy Display Systems Ltd
Fircroft Way
Edenbridge
Kent
TN8 6ET
☎ 0732 863666

Supertube
Aercon Works
Alfred Road
Gravesend
Kent
DA11 7QF
☎ 0474 564177

Syma Systems (UK)
Portland Trading Estate
Low Moor Road
Kirkby-in-Ashfield
Nottingham
NG17 7LF
☎ 0623 754903

System 8
Unit 4
Wellington Road
London
SW19 8EQ
☎ 081 879 3272

System Freestyle Ltd
Unit 8
Cirrus Court
Glebe Road
Huntingdon
Cambs.
PE18 7DX
☎ 0480 420071

Systemworks Ltd
Unit 12
Watford Enterprise Centre
Greenhill Crescent
Watford
WD1 8XU
☎ 0923 248399

Tower Display PLC
Head Office: Tower House
Towcester Road
London
E3 3ND
☎ 071 538 9995

Trigostruct Ltd
P.O. Box 37
Luton
LU1 1XB
☎ 0528 453308

Voluma Connector Systems
12 Brentford Business Centre
Commerce Road
Brentford
TW8 8LG
☎ 081 569 9742

GLOSSARY

AEO	Association of Exhibition Organisers.
Aisle	Gangway between blocks of exhibition stands
Ambient light	The natural light available.
Annual	Exhibition held every year.
Applied graphics	Non-removable words and pictures applied directly to the stand structure or panels.
Audience	The visitors attending an exhibition.
Audio-visual	Equipment used to produce sound or present pictures (slides or film) used on the stand.
Audit	A verification of the numbers of visitors attending an exhibition. Only really valid if carried out by an independent specialist organisation.
BECA	British Exhibition Contractors Association.
BEVA	British Exhibition Venues Association.
Bi-annual	Exhibition held twice a year.
Bi-ennial	Exhibition held every two years.
Bonded warehouse/site	An area within which imported goods can be stored or displayed without payment of the normal customs duty.
Booth	American word for exhibition stand.
BOTB	British Overseas Trade Board.
Break-down	Period within which stands are dismantled at the end of an exhibition.
Brief	Instructions given to designer or contractor.
Build-up	Period within which stands are erected prior to the start of an exhibition.
Buzz-bars	Heavy duty metal bars distributing electrical current throughout an exhibition hall.
Carnet	Document needed to move parts from one country to another.
Carry-card	(USA) A card designed to award the recipient a prize when bought to the stand.

Catalogue	A printed listing of exhibits.
CCTV	Closed circuit television.
Chippy	Slang word for exhibition carpenter.
Clearance	Measurement of clear space, usually above a stand.
Closed shop	Agreement whereby only members of a trade union were allowed to work in exhibition halls. Now illegal.
Competition law	Laws of EC forbidding the exclusion of competitive organisations, especially foreign, from exhibitions.
Consolidation	Collecting of freight from a number of exhibitors and shipping in one batch.
Consumer event	Exhibition aimed at members of the public.
Contractor	Supplier of services to exhibitors and organisers.
Customs seal	Seal applied by customs officers to vehicles travelling from one bonded area to another.
Deadline dates	Dates by which work has to be completed, or orders placed.
Display graphics	Portable signs and words/pictures designed to be used on a stand and temporarily affixed or placed.
Double-decker	A two-storey stand.
Double-sided tape	Tape applying a strip of adhesive to a surface, and having an exposed adhesive surface uppermost.
Drayage	(USA) Movement of goods between the exhibition hall loading bay and the site in the exhibition hall.
DTI	Department of Trade and Industry.
Exclusive contract	(USA) An agreement whereby only one contractor is allowed to work on an exhibition, or in an exhibition hall (see Tied contract).
Exhibit Manager	(USA) The individual appointed by an exhibiting organisation to oversee the participation in exhibitions.
Exhibitor	An organisation participating in an exhibition.
Failure to vacate	Insurance term denoting an exhibitor's failure to dismantle the stand and remove it from the hall within the agreed time.
Fascia	The headboard of a stand, carrying the name of the company.
Flame-proofed	Material which has been chemically treated to render it fire retardant.
Floor-plan	Printed layout of stands in an exhibition hall.
Fluorescent	A fluorescent light tube, sometimes called a 'florrie'.

Footfall	The number of visitors passing a stand.
Free-build	A stand built by an exhibitor on floor space only, as opposed to a shell-scheme.
Frontage	The side(s) of a stand nearest to passing visitors.
Gangway	Aisle.
Give-aways	Gifts, usually printed with a company name, distributed to visitors.
Graphics	Words and pictures on a stand.
Hall-owners	The management of an exhibition hall.
Header	(USA) Fascia.
Heatsealing	Method by which graphics can be sealed under clear plastic sheet.
Hold harmless	(USA) Legal term meaning to absolve from responsibility.
Inserts	Printed advertising material placed between pages of magazine or catalogue. Also called 'free-standing inserts' in USA.
Island site	A site for a stand which is open on all four sides.
Joint venture	Arrangement between trade association and DTI to participate in overseas exhibition with DTI subsidy.
Juice	Slang for electrical current.
Landscape	The presentation of a picture with the long edges horizontal (see also 'Portrait').
Light batten	Strut to which lights are fixed.
Light box	Box structure used to provide a back-lit graphic.
Listing allowances	Term used by contractors for commissions paid to organisers and hall-owners on sales of goods and services ordered by exhibitors.
Loading (floor)	Maximum weight that may be placed on the floor of an exhibition hall.
Loading (electrical)	The amount of electrical power required by electrical equipment on the stand. Expressed in kilowatts.
Logo	Company trade-mark.
Loop nylon	Fabric often used for panels providing a surface to which velcro tape can grip.
Manual	Collection of exhibition information, rules and regulations and order forms for services. Published by organiser and sent to exhibitors booking stands at the exhibition.

Modular display	Exhibition display systems using components that can be built into a number of different shaped and sized configurations.
MMC	Monopolies and Mergers Commission.
Monitors	Computer or TV screens.
Monopoly	Exclusive and profitable supply of product or service, an arrangement common in the exhibition industry.
Montage	Artistic layout of individual components to provide a visually attractive display piece.
Muslin	Light woven mesh fabric commonly used for exhibition stand ceilings.
NAEH	National Association of Exhibition Halls.
Nameboard	Fascia.
NEA	National Exhibitors Association.
Night sheets	Sheets stretched across the front of an exhibition stand overnight, to discourage theft.
OFT	Office of Fair Trading.
Organiser	The arranger of the exhibition.
Package deal	Arrangement offered to exhibitors whereby a range of services (furniture hire, electrical, etc) can be purchased for an all-in price.
Panels	Sheets of material used to form the walls of a stand.
Pipe and draipe	(USA) Structure of metal tubes and fabric used to provide a low-cost light-weight booth area.
Platform/plinth	Raised area on which stand can be erected. Used to hide pipes and cables, and to emphasise stand.
Portrait	The presentation of a picture with the long edges vertical (see also 'Landscape').
Porter	Contractor transporting goods within exhibition hall.
Pre-registration	The registration of potential visitors to the exhibition prior to opening.
Press office	Office at exhibition where journalists can collect press kits, make telephone calls etc.
Press kits/pack	Collection of information for the press, put together by exhibitors.
Public exhibition	Event aimed at the general public.
Preview/review	An editorial description of an exhibition and its exhibits, published in a trade magazine.

Puff	An editorial mention of the show, or a preview, published by a trade magazine, often in exchange for advertising or other favours.
Punters	Slang term for exhibitors or visitors used by organisers.
Security	Arrangements made at exhibition to minimise theft.
Service desk	Desk staffed by contractor's representative during build-up.
Setting up	Build-up.
Shell scheme	Temporary structure erected by organiser to provide exhibitors with back and side walls and a fascia.
Show management	(USA) Organiser.
Sight lines	Views of the exhibition stand as seen by the visitor.
Site	The area on which an exhibition is held, or a stand erected.
Site manager	A contractors representative on-site at an exhibition.
Space/stand space	The area sold to an exhibitor.
Space only	Floor space only sold, as opposed to space with shell-scheme.
Sparks	Slang for electrician.
Spot	Slang for spotlight.
Stand	The exhibit.
Stand manager	Manager appointed by the exhibitor to take charge of the running of the stand.
Sub-contractor	Contractor hired by another contractor to perform part of total job.
Subbed out	Sub-contracted.
Table-top event	Low cost exhibition using tables for stands.
Talking head	Visual attraction whereby a film of someone talking is projected onto a plaster cast of their face to provide a lifelike illustion.
Tear-down	(USA) Break-down.
Tenancy	Period that an organiser occupies an exhibition hall including build-up, show days and break-down.
Thematic stand	A stand with a theme.
Tie bars	Struts used to strengthen stand structures.

Tied contract	Monopolistic arrangement favoured by many exhibition hall-owners, organisers and contractors whereby exhibitors are required to buy services from only one contractor, often at very high prices.
Track	Continuous insulated strip into which a number of lights can be fitted.
Trade show	(USA) An exhibition for a trade or industry, as opposed to the public.
Traffic	Visitors to an exhibition.
Tranny	Slang for transparency.
Trust	(USA) Monopoly.
Tyre-kicker	(USA) Slang for any visitor who is perceived as a non-buyer.
Van lines	(USA) Transportation companies.
Velcro	Trade name for tape containing tiny plastic hooks which grip on contact with loop nylon. Used extensively by exhibitors for mounting graphics.
Venue	Exhibition hall.
Visitor promotion	Publicity carried out by organiser to attract visitors to exhibition.
Visual	Full colour drawing of an exhibition stand shown to exhibitor by designer. First rough visuals are called 'scamps'.
Water and waste	Slang for plumbing on an exhibition stand.
Z accounts	Accounting method by which commission earned by organisers or hall-owners on exhibitors' purchasers is credited to a confidential account out of which cash, or payments for gifts can be drawn by the beneficiary.

LIST OF FURTHER READING

Alles, Alfred. *Exhibitions: A key to effective marketing*, Cassell, 2nd ed. 1988

Northover, John. *The Exhibitors Handbook*, Kogan Page, 1990

Talbot, John. *How to make exhibitions work for your business*: Kogan Page 1989

Hoshen, Nathan. *Planning and running your exhibition stand*: Management Update 1988

Black, Sam. *Exhibitions and Conferences from A–Z*: The Modino Press Ltd 1989

Miller, Steve. *How to get the most out of trade shows*: NTC Business Books (USA) 1990

Chapman, Edward A. *Exhibit Marketing*: McGrewottill Book Co (USA) 1987

Allwood, John and Bryan Montgomery. *Exhibition planning and design*, BT Batsford Ltd 1989

Waterhouse, David. *Making the most of exhibitions*, Gower Publishing Co Ltd 1987

INDEX